Mexico Inside Out

Praise for this book

'The richness and complexity of Mexican history, politics, and culture made extraordinarily readable without simplification. A great introduction to Mexico.'

Professor Jenny Pearce, Latin America and Caribbean Centre,
London School of Economics

'A readable and deeply informed guide to contemporary Mexico, its dramas and its beauty.'

David Lehmann, Centre for Latin American Studies,
Cambridge University

'Nick Caistor offers us a brilliant synthesis that, in a fluid and attractive style, takes us through the history, culture, and social life of Mexicans and helps us understand the mysteries of the current political situation.'

Roger Bartra, author of
The Cage of Melancholy

LATIN AMERICA BUREAU (LAB)

LAB is an independent charitable organisation, based in London, which provides news, analysis and information on Latin America, reporting consistently from the perspective of the region's poor, oppressed or marginalized communities and social movements. LAB brings an alternative, critical awareness and understanding of Latin America to readers throughout the English-speaking world. LAB is widely known for its books and operates a website, updated daily, in which it carries news and analysis on Latin America and reports from our partners and correspondents in the region (www.lab.org.uk).

Mexico Inside Out

People, politics and culture

Nick Caistor

Published by Practical Action Publishing Ltd and Latin America Bureau

Practical Action Publishing Ltd
27a Albert Street, Rugby, Warwickshire, CV21 2SG, UK
www.practicalactionpublishing.com

Latin America Bureau
Enfield House, Castle Street, Clun, Shropshire, SY7 8JU, UK
www.lab.org.uk

A catalogue record for this book is available from the British Library.

A catalogue record for this book has been requested from the Library of Congress.

9781788531771 Paperback
9781788531788 Hardback
9781788531801 eBook

Citation: Caistor, N. (2021) *Mexico Inside Out: People, politics and culture*, Rugby,
UK: Practical Action Publishing <http://dx.doi.org/10.3362/9781788531801>.

Since 1974, Practical Action Publishing has published and disseminated books
and information in support of international development work throughout
the world. Practical Action Publishing is a trading name of Practical Action
Publishing Ltd (Company Reg. No. 1159018), the wholly owned publishing
company of Practical Action. Practical Action Publishing trades only in support
of its parent charity objectives and any profits are covenanted back to Practical
Action (Charity Reg. No. 247257, Group VAT Registration No. 880 9924 76).

Latin America Bureau (Research and Action) Limited is a UK registered charity
(no. 1113039). Since 1977 LAB has been publishing books, news, analysis and
information about Latin America, reporting consistently from the perspective of the
region's poor, oppressed or marginalized communities and social movements. In
2015 LAB entered into a publishing partnership with Practical Action Publishing.

Cover image credit: Fernando Soto Vidal
Typeset by JMR Digital, India

Contents

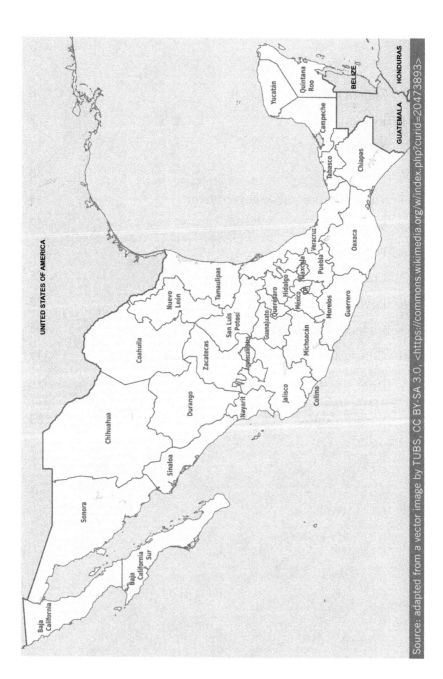

1 Introduction

The 1st of December 2018 saw the start of what many Mexicans hoped would be a peaceful revolution. This was the day when Andres Manuel López Obrador took office as president. For the first time, the new head of state did not belong to one of the two main parties that have alternated in power in Mexico since 2000: the PRI (Partido de la Revolución Institucional or Institutional Revolutionary Party), which held power for more than 70 years, and the PAN (Partido de Acción Nacional, or National Action Party).

AMLO, as he is widely known, is head of the MORENA movement (Movimiento de Regeneración Nacional, or Movement of National Regeneration), a grouping of left, centrist and right-wing forces that became a properly constituted political party only a few years previously, in 2014. López Obrador was no newcomer to the political fray: he had to struggle hard for many years to reach the presidency. Starting out on the left wing of the PRI, he joined forces with Cuauhtèmoc Cárdenas, the son of the legendary 1930s nationalist leader Lázaro Cárdenas, when Cuauhtemoc was robbed of victory by fraud in the 1988 presidential election. He went on to join him in founding the PRD (Partido de la Revolución Democrática, the Democratic Revolutionary Party) in 1989. Cárdenas became the first elected *jefe de gobierno* of the capital, Mexico City, in the mid-1990s, but lost the presidential vote again in 2000. AMLO followed him as the political leader of Mexico City, a key position in Mexican politics.

At the end of his term as mayor, he began to garner support to stand as the PRD's candidate for the 2006 presidential election. When after several days' delay, the PAN candidate Felipe Calderón was declared to have won by a mere 0.56 per cent, AMLO refused to accept the result. Styling himself the 'legitimate president of Mexico' for several months he led massive demonstrations in the capital and elsewhere attempting to have the result overturned. On 20 November 2006 in an event in Mexico City's Zócalo, thousands of his supporters 'inaugurated' him as president and he announced the creation of an 'alternative cabinet'.

Little by little, however, these protests began to fade, and AMLO returned to building up grassroots support and turning his attention to winning in 2012. Claiming he wanted to create the *república amorosa'* ('a loving republic') and to encourage *'abrazos no balazos'* ('hugs not bullets') in response to Felipe Calderón's aggressive stance in combating drug violence, he stood once more as the PRD candidate in a coalition named the 'Movimiento Progresista' (Progressive Movement).

This time when he lost by more than 7 per cent to the PRI's Enrique Peña Nieto, AMLO again cried foul, but was unable to muster the same popular support as on the previous occasion. As a result, he announced he was quitting the PRD to set up the MORENA movement. When AMLO stood a third time in the July 2018 presidential election, it was as part of the Junto Haremos Historia (Together We'll Make History) coalition which included MORENA, the Partido de los Trabajadores (Workers' Party) on the left, and the right-wing Encuentro Social (Social Encounter Party). This time he emerged the clear winner.

Only a little more than three decades before AMLO took office, the Peruvian Nobel Prize winning author Mario Vargas Llosa described Mexico as the 'perfect dictatorship' due to the stranglehold the PRI had on state power at all levels. In 1988, it is generally acknowledged that the PRI committed widespread fraud to ensure its candidate Carlos Salinas de Gortari was awarded the presidency, to the detriment of Cuauhtemoc Cárdenas. This appears to have been the PRI's last-ditch effort to retain control of Mexico's political institutions as it had done since the 1930s. By the 1990s, Mexico and the world around it had undergone many fundamental changes.

During Salinas's period in office, he began to open up the Mexican economy, selling off many state monopolies and revoking the sacred Agrarian Reform that underpinned the PRI's legitimacy. The most notorious example of this was the dismantling of the monopoly on communications, as mobile telephony boomed. The main concessions were snapped up by the already immensely wealthy businessman Carlos Slim, making him one of the richest men in the world according to the *Forbes* magazine annual list. Thanks to having a protected monopoly following the privatization of Teléfonos de México in 1991, Slim's fortune rose from US$3.7 billion to $6.1 billion between 1994 and 1995.

The North American Free Trade Agreement

The main goal of Salinas' economic policy was to align Mexico ever more closely with the United States and to a lesser extent Canada. Following lengthy negotiations, this led to the signing of the North American Free Trade Agreement (NAFTA) between the three countries on 1 January 1994. This was aimed at ensuring Mexico would become part of the developed 'first world', helping its economy converge with the others, creating jobs and encouraging investment from the two countries to the north.

In fact, the opposite happened, making the divergence between Mexico and its northern neighbours even more pronounced. The promised economic growth failed to materialize: instead, Mexico became the home for low-paid *maquila* jobs producing cheap goods for the US market.

Wages in Mexico stagnated: the average weekly pay of a Mexican worker remained equivalent to what a US worker could earn in a single day. Mexico's subsistence farmers found it impossible to compete against subsidized exports from the USA. An estimated 2 million peasant farmers and rural workers lost their livelihoods, while the country's small and medium-sized companies also found it hard to rival their more efficient northern competitors. Investment from the north was concentrated in a very few sectors, most notably car manufacturing and assembly for major US companies, as well as large-scale Canadian mining companies. In the banking and finance sectors, a year after the signing of the agreement, foreign companies operating in Mexico enjoyed profits equivalent to more than 40 per cent of total profits in the sector.

In general, NAFTA led to the Mexican economy becoming increasingly reliant on the United States. More than 85 per cent of its exports now go to its northern neighbour, making Mexico extremely vulnerable to any shock to the US economy. This was evident during the worldwide 2008–2009 economic crisis, which affected Mexico far more than any other Latin American country. Similarly in 2020, the COVID-19 pandemic is likely to have disastrous consequences both economically and socially in Mexico. Not only will its exports be badly hit, but millions of newly unemployed Mexicans living in the United States are likely to return home, leading to higher levels of unemployment and greatly reducing the valuable remittances they usually send back.

The Zapatista uprising

Nor did NAFTA do much to resolve the problem of emigration from the poor south of Mexico to the north of the country and the United States. Almost half the Mexican population has remained below the poverty line, the majority of them in southern states such as Oaxaca, Chiapas, and the Yucatán. The indigenous populations here are not only among the poorest of all Mexicans, but they continue to suffer discrimination and a lack of respect for their different traditions.

The dangers of this neglect became evident on the day that NAFTA came into force, 1 January 1994. This was when the Zapatista Army of National Liberation (EZLN in its Spanish acronym), led an indigenous uprising in the Lacandón jungle in the Chiapas highlands. Several thousand indigenous people took over several towns, led by their charismatic spokesman Subcomandante Marcos, a non-indigenous philosophy graduate from the Autonomous University of Mexico. The Zapatistas were protesting against the federal government's repeal of Article 27 of the 1917 revolutionary constitution, which guaranteed the rights of local rural communities or *ejidos* to own land communally, as well as demanding greater autonomy for the indigenous people not only of their immediate region, but throughout Mexico.

The Zapatista insurrection was seen as the most serious threat in many years to the Mexican state, and the government responded by sending as many as 20,000 troops to quell the revolt. The fighting between the two sides went on for several days, and resulted in at least 300 indigenous deaths. After the Zapatistas withdrew from the towns and villages they had taken over, a truce was called.

It took more than two years for the government and the Zapatistas to reach an agreement to end hostilities, known as the San Andres accord. This agreement promised greater respect for indigenous autonomy, land ownership, and diversity. The terms of the San Andres agreement were supposed to be enshrined in modifications to Mexico's national constitution, but Zedillo's PRI government did nothing to implement this, and the problem was left for Vicente Fox to resolve. In March 2001, the Zapatistas organized a two-week march from Chiapas to Mexico City, gathering more than 100,000 supporters along the way, to make sure the Fox administration kept its promise to amend the constitution. These changes were meant to guarantee indigenous rights to communal land ownership, as well as greater autonomy in making their own laws and self-government, but in fact little has changed in the treatment of this historically oppressed part of the Mexican population.

With NAFTA failing to provide the promised miraculous boost to the Mexican economy, and the Zapatistas and other civil society groups demonstrating how much social unrest was simmering just below the surface, it came as no great surprise when for the first time in more than 70 years, the PRI lost power at the 2000 presidential and legislative elections.

The PAN in power

The new president was Vicente Fox, leader of the right-wing PAN, whose earlier career as head of Coca Cola in Mexico was symbolic of the changing political and social climate in the new millennium. Many local observers consider that as president, Vicente Fox did little to seize the opportunity to foster real democratic participation. He preferred, as the old political adage has it, to change a few things in order for everything to stay the same. It was the PAN's turn to get their hands on the honey pot, and they proved almost as corrupt, nepotistic and authoritarian as their PRI predecessors. During President Fox's six-year term in office, little effort was made to reform the vast state apparatus built up by the PRI over many decades, while the same neo-liberal economic policies it had pursued in the 1990s were stepped up by his administration.

The PRI was defeated a second time in the 2006 elections, when once again the PAN candidate, Felipe Calderón, was elected to the presidency, by a wafer-thin majority. These two successive failures led some to predict that the PRI itself would splinter and even fade away entirely, as it no longer responded to most Mexicans' needs As one joker put it at the time: 'PRI=RIP'. However, Calderón's six years as head of government showed that whatever changes might have taken place at the top level of politics, the social problems besetting Mexico were still unresolved. President Calderón made some timid attempts to reform the most blatantly inadequate parts of the system, such as the judiciary and pensions, but his presidency will be remembered for one thing above all: the open war he declared on the illegal drugs trade.

The war on drug cartels

The crisis of violence caused by illegal drug production and trafficking had grown considerably worse through the 1990s and the early 2000s. After the death of the Colombian drug lord Pablo Escobar and the disintegration of the Medellín and Cali drug cartels, Mexican gangs largely took over the supply of cocaine, heroin and other drugs to the United States and Europe. Their violent methods, plus the obvious corruption of the many different police forces and officials, from local mayors to state governors, led President Calderón to 'declare war' on the Mexican drug cartels. He brought in the armed forces – often the navy marines – to take on the traffickers, with the goal of capturing the ringleaders to disrupt their gangs' activities, and hand them over to the US authorities. This strategy led to a sharp spike in deaths and disappearances, which reached an estimated 120,000 by the end of his six-year term in office. Although President Calderón did make attempts to reform the judiciary and to develop a coherent environmental strategy, the upsurge in violence made his government so unpopular that the next elections in 2012 helped bring about the resurrection of the PRI.

Their candidate, Enrique Peña Nieto, was an ambitious 46 year old who had previously been a popular governor of the State of Mexico, the most densely populated state in the country. He was elected on a wave of optimism that this new generation of PRI leaders could use the party's heritage to improve things in a way that Calderón had struggled to do. President Peña Nieto began by calling on the opposition parties to join him in a pact to bring in widespread reforms. However, the optimism and enthusiasm soon evaporated, as he proved as incapable as his predecessor at providing answers to the country's pressing problems. Violence surrounding the illegal drugs trade continued and even worsened.

One particular case, that of the 2014 disappearance and presumed deaths of 43 students from an agricultural college in Ayotzinapa, near the town of Iguala in the state of Guerrero, suggested that little had changed. Although the exact details will never be clear, it appears the local police handed the students over to a drugs gang, who murdered them all. Their bodies have never been found and identified. It soon emerged that not only was the town of Iguala's mayor directly involved, but the state governor as well. The subsequent failure by the federal authorities properly to investigate these deaths, and the fact that nobody directly involved was ever brought to trial (only 3 per cent of murders in Mexico ever lead to a suspected perpetrator having to face justice) led many to conclude that President Peña Nieto's claim to represent a new, squeaky clean version of the PRI was so much hot air.

Alongside this, little came of the president's promised reforms of the judicial system, education, pensions, and of state industries such as the oil company PEMEX. His attempts to open up the oil industry to foreign competition was seen as a threat to PEMEX's cosseted army of managers and employees, and met with fierce resistance. Peña Nieto and his wife also became embroiled in allegations of corruption over housing contracts and influence peddling. As a result, for the second half of his six-year term, the PRI leader came to be seen as a lame-duck president with little support even within his own party.

By the time of the July 2018 national elections, therefore, both main political parties were largely discredited in the eyes of Mexico's 90 million voters. This provided Andres Manuel López Obrador with a big opportunity. During his energetic campaign crisscrossing the country, he stressed time and again that he represented real change in Mexico, with a political programme that appealed to the young as well as the poorer and indigenous sectors. In the event, he secured a sweeping victory in the polls, winning more than 53 per cent of the vote in the first round. His MORENA party also gained majorities in both houses of the federal congress, and won 31 out of 32 state governorships.

Mexico's 'fourth transformation'

In December 2018, the hard work began, as AMLO embarked on this 'fourth transformation' of Mexico. He identified the first three as Mexico's declaration of independence from Spain in 1821; the great liberal reforms of the 1860s that saw limits put on the power of the Catholic Church and the strengthening of civilian rule over the military; and the 1910 Revolution that created modern Mexico. What the new president proposed was 'not only a change of government, but a change of the political system'. In his inaugural speech he declared that 'neoliberal economic policies have been a disaster, a calamity for public life...Privatization in Mexico has been synonymous with corruption...' His main test so far has been to find a way to reform the state so that it can act as the promoter of a fairer society with less disparity in wealth and more opportunities of all kinds, without falling back into the discredited state monopolization of public institutions and economic power as exercised for so many years by the PRI.

In addition to these deep-seated transformations, AMLO has had to attempt to maintain Mexico's economic stability in difficult times; to try to lift many millions of Mexicans out of poverty; level up development between the north and south of the country; deal with the continuing crisis of migrants from central America trying to cross Mexico to reach the United States; find a way to stem the violence arising in the main from illegal drug trafficking, but also the increasing wave of femicides. And last but not least, to deal with the administration of Donald J. Trump in Washington.

The 21st century has seen great political, social, and economic changes in Mexico. By the dawn of the millennium, a political system that had evolved and prospered over decades had fallen apart. Over the past two decades, Mexicans have been able to enjoy far greater democratic choice in who they wish to govern them. This opening up of society has led to many more groups organizing protests and social media campaigns to make their presence felt by the politicians. The challenge for AMLO's administration, as well as the opposition parties, is to offer a coherent ideology and clear ideas about how to resolve the country's many pressing problems. With half its 130 million population still under 30, the greatest test lies in finding ways to combine economic development with a more open, pluralistic society in which fewer of its people are left behind in poverty, without a voice.

Mexico City's Angel of Independence (Valeria Arendar)

2 The land

'Poor Mexico! So far from God and so near to the United States.' This heartfelt cry from the 19th-century dictator Porfirio Díaz sums up Mexico's dilemma: how can it thrive and progress when it shares a 3,000-kilometre border with the most economically advanced country on the planet? When the Spaniards created the viceroyalty of New Spain in the 16th century, its territory extended far into what is now the northern neighbour: California, New Mexico, Texas, Arizona, and Florida were all part of Spain's largest and richest colony. Mexico won independence from Spain only three decades after its northern neighbour cut its ties with Great Britain, but as the United States progressed and industrialized through the next two centuries, for many reasons, Mexico fell behind.

The two worlds collide at the rivers on Mexico's northern border, the Rio Colorado flowing west into the Gulf of California, and the Rio Bravo, or the Rio Grande as the gringos call it, which flows east. For many years, Mexicans in search of a better income and a more secure way of life have crossed these rivers into the United States. At times, they have been welcomed, as during the Second World War when the *bracero* scheme brought in many thousands of Mexican seasonal workers to replace US workers called up to fight. At others, they have been regarded with suspicion, refused residence permits, and deported back across to Mexico. In recent years Mexican migrants have been joined by thousands from the central American countries of Guatemala, El Salvador, and Honduras, who are also seeking to flee economic instability and violent crime in their own countries. These migrants are often taken across the hot northern deserts of Mexico to the Rio Bravo, crossing it on inflated rubber tyres or other flimsy craft, then into more desert land on the other side. They hope that by getting into the United States (Texas, Arizona, or other border states) they can then either disappear northwards without papers or wait to be picked up by the US Border Patrol (the feared *migra* or migration agents) and apply for asylum, although this has become increasingly rare.

As many as half a million migrants also make the dangerous journey through Mexico every year to reach this northern border on freight trains known as *La Bestia* (The Beast) or *el tren de la muerte* (the train of death). This network of trains stretches from the southern border with Guatemala up to villages like Altar in Sonora, some ninety kilometres from the US frontier. Here the migrants from Mexico and Central America have to wait while the US authorities process their asylum applications. The number of those accepted has fallen dramatically since January 2019, when the Mexican government accepted the Trump administration's campaign to push for them to 'remain in Mexico'. Nowadays, close to 90 per cent of the applications are rejected.

Apart from the rivers, the most visible sign of the border is the infamous Wall built to deter as many people as possible from entering the USA. Partially begun in the 1990s, Donald

The border near Tijuana (Tomás Castelazo)

Trump boasted during his 2016 presidential campaign that he was going to 'build the wall' all the way from Tijuana in the West to Brownsville (Matamoros) in the Gulf of Mexico – and get the Mexicans to pay for it. So far only about an additional hundred kilometres have been built – and the US taxpayer has funded it.

Seven of Mexico's 32 states occupy the land close to this northern frontier. Baja California (North and South) is a mostly arid peninsula more than 1,300 kilometres long but only 160 kilometres wide. Sparsely populated, it attracts tourists for its abundant sea life and picturesque bays. On the western mainland, the lowlands and deserts of Sonora and Sinaloa extend up into the southern United States. The land here is becoming increasingly parched due to over-exploitation and climate change, creating increasing problems for the many small farmers. Proximity to the United States also means these areas have become important staging posts for shipping illegal drugs north, often through Pacific coastal ports such as Lázaro Cárdenas. Every month, lengthy tunnels are discovered, through which people and drugs are smuggled into United States' territory.

Mountains and minerals

The cordillera of the Sierra Madre forms the mountainous backbone to these northern regions. These mountains once boasted dense forests that were the home of indigenous groups such as the Yaqui and Tarahumara. These peoples long resisted attempts to impose rule by the central government hundreds of kilometres away, but as the forests have been cleared, so their traditional way of life has become increasingly threatened. The Sierra Madre has for centuries provided Mexico with its mineral wealth. Gold, silver, copper, and tin mines are dotted throughout the landscape, nowadays many of them in foreign, largely Canadian, ownership.

Between the two branches of the Sierra Madre lies the plateau or Mesa Norte, stretching from Chihuahua (the largest of Mexico's 32 states) down to the silver city of San Luis Potosí. On the *mesa's* western slopes, deep rivers flowing down to the Pacific Ocean have cut deep valleys such as the famous Barranca del Cobre (Copper Canyon), well-known these days for its spectacular tourist train ride.

Life on the border

More recent wealth is a characteristic of the eastern border area in the state of Nuevo León. The state capital Monterrey is the richest and most technologically advanced city in Mexico. Its population growth, from less than half a million in 1950 to close to 5 million in 2020 gives some idea of its dynamism. It is the centre for many industries, above all in the hi-tech sector, which benefits from the Monterrey Institute of Technology, attracting students from all over the country. This institute was founded by Eduardo Garza Sada, from a family that began in business as brewers at the end of the 19th century, but is now a huge concern, owning companies from petrochemicals to automobiles. Monterrey is also a very Catholic, conservative city, known as a stronghold of the right-wing PAN political party.

Being close to the border has meant that other cities like Ciudad Juarez, Tijuana, and Matamoros have also experienced rapid growth. First developed in the 1930s by President Lázaro Cárdenas as a way to counterbalance US influence in the border region, they are now the hub for the many hundreds of *maquila* plants that have sprung up since the 1970s, assembly-line factories producing finished garments and other products from components shipped in from the United States, and then re-exported back there. These border cities often suffer from a chronic lack of proper infrastructure, with insufficient schools, hospitals, and roads. Many of the migrants from the south of Mexico flock here for work and are forced to live in poor shanty towns where violence, especially against women, is rife.

Volcanoes and earthquakes

Further south, a central volcanic plateau dominates the landscape. The *meseta* stretches through Michoácan, Hidalgo, Jalisco and the state of Mexico. The Orizaba or Citlalépetl volcano at the southern end is the highest point in Mexico at 5,610 metres. Equally famous are the two volcanoes closer to the capital (and visible from it on a clear day if the smog has lifted) Popocatépetl (5,465 metres high) and Iztaccihuatl (5,230 metres). This chain of volcanoes is still active, and includes one of the world's youngest volcanoes, Paricutín. In 1943, a local farmer heard underground rumblings for several days, and then noticed that a small conical volcano a few metres high had sprouted in one of his maize fields. Lava from it soon engulfed the nearby village of Paricutín, and the volcano continued to throw out lava for eight or more years until it reached a height of more than 3,000 metres.

These volcanoes and the earthquakes that stem from Mexico being on the edge between the North American tectonic plate and the Pacific plate shaped the religious beliefs of many of Mexico's ancient civilizations, who saw these natural phenomena as signs of an unstable universe at war with itself. Over the centuries, volcanic eruptions and seismic activity have caused many tragedies and great loss of life, most recently in the huge 1985 earthquake which caused as many as 10,000 deaths in Mexico City, with thousands more left homeless. A second, less damaging earthquake hit the capital exactly 32 years after the first one.

Capital and megalopolis

Mexico's capital in the centre of the Valley of Mexico was built on the ruins of the Aztec Tenochtitlán. Both cities were at the heart of empires, and today Mexico City (Distrito Federal) remains at the heart of Mexican life. Under Spanish colonial rule, it was the biggest and richest city in the Americas, the administrative and political hub for the vast territories of New Spain, which stretched from what is now the state of Oregon in the United States' north-west to the Straits of Darien in the south. By the end of the 19th century when the dictator Porfirio Díaz modernized the country and encouraged foreign investment, it has been estimated that more than a third of all industry was concentrated in the capital, and nearly all of the investment was directed there. Much of the wealth from Mexico's mines and agriculture also ended up here, and the richest families displayed their affluence in palaces, culture, and fashion, as well as their appetite for imported goods.

Throughout the 20th century, the capital's population continued to grow enormously as each new economic crisis drove thousands of poor Mexicans from the countryside to the city in search of employment, and many more were attracted by the opportunity to succeed in business, politics, or the arts. By the 1970s, some 14 million people lived in what was then known as the Distrito Federal and surrounding areas. The built-up area spread far beyond its original boundaries into the hills surrounding the valley, where new *colonías* peopled by recent migrants sprang up. The population is now estimated at more than 20 million, with the city's 16 *delegaciones* or boroughs ringed by new urban centres in the state of Mexico such as Nezahualcóyotl or Ecatepec, which themselves have more than a million inhabitants.

The Mexican capital is a city of huge contrasts, with luxury neighbourhoods like Polanco or Las Lomas cheek by jowl with some of the poorest. As in other Latin American capitals, the old colonial centre with its historic churches and palaces was for years run-down and considered dangerous, but at the turn of the 21st century the then city mayor López Obrador formed a surprising partnership with the telecoms billionaire Carlos Slim to clean up and improve security in the centre around the Zócalo. This square, formally known as the Plaza de la

The restored Alameda in Mexico City's historic centre (Nick Caistor)

Constitución, is lined by the Aztec Templo Mayor, the Spanish colonial cathedral, the presidential palace and City Hall. The Zócalo is the place where, for century after century, the destinies of Mexico's men and women have been decided. It is here that thousands gather in September each year to celebrate the 'Grito de Dolores' that marked the start of the struggle for independence from Spain, and here that all the big political acts and protests take place.

The sheer size of the capital creates many problems, from chronic air pollution to everyday crime and the difficulties in getting around the city. Crossing from one side to another can take more than three hours, especially during rush hours. The French-designed metro system carries millions of passengers into and out of the centre every day, while a recent network of rapid Metro buses has also slightly helped ease the traffic congestion.

Colonial splendour

In the region beyond the Valley of Mexico, the rich volcanic soil and more plentiful rainfall has made the area known as El Bajío the breadbasket of Mexico, as wheat and maize are grown on large farms to supply the capital and other cities like the second biggest city, Guadalajara, with a population of more than 5 million. The locals, or *tapatíos* as they like to be known, consider their city to be the heartland of Mexico: this is where the *charros* or Mexican cowboys are from, together with *mariachi* music and the production of tequila. More than half of Mexico's estimated 129 million people live in this central region, and this is where elegant colonial cities like Puebla, Tasco, and Querétaro are to be found. As the plateau slopes down to the Pacific in the west, the coastline is home to famous tourist resorts such as Acapulco, Puerto Vallarta, and Puerto Escondido.

To the east of this central *meseta* lies the coastal plain of the Gulf of Mexico, stretching 1500 kilometres down from Tamaulipas on the Texan border through the states of Veracruz and Tabasco to the Yucatán peninsula. This is where Mexico's oil industry is concentrated. The first oil well was drilled onshore near Tampico in 1901, and more recent discoveries in the Gulf of Mexico have seen the port of Veracruz prosper. Veracruz is the traditional centre of this region. It was founded by Hernán Cortés,

Colonial calm in San Miguel de Allende (Lucia Caistor)

who named it Villa Rica de la Vera Cruz, as he landed there on Good Friday 1519. Ever since, it has been Mexico's main link with Europe, at least until the coming of the aeroplane. The first railway was built from the capital in 1873, and the port has always welcomed visitors and immigrants, among them the thousands of refugees fleeing the Spanish Civil War at the end of the 1930s. It was also here that black slaves were brought to work in the nearby sugar plantations, with the result that Mexico became second only to Brazil in Latin America for the number of imported African slaves. Because of their geographical position and the racially mixed population, Veracruzanos regard themselves as more cosmopolitan and outward-looking than the inhabitants of the capital.

The southern states

The two southernmost states, Oaxaca to the west and Chiapas to the east, are also the poorest. It is here that the indigenous presence is strongest, and these groups have historically felt that the governments in the distant federal capital have done little to improve their lives. There have been frequent recent conflicts in Oaxaca, but it was the January 1994 uprising in the Lacandón jungle in Chiapas, led by the Zapatista EZLN army, that brought the plight of the local indigenous population to national and international attention. Since then, successive administrations have produced plans to improve regional infrastructure and provide employment in the region, usually to little effect. The latest scheme, launched by President López Obrador soon after he came to power at the end of 2018, is the proposed 1500 kilometre long Tren Maya (Mayan Train), touted by the government as an opportunity to bring more tourism and trade to Chiapas and the Yucatán peninsula. But it is much criticized for the ecological damage it will do.

This peninsula, with its dry limestone *karst* landscape, dotted with sudden sinkholes or *cenotes*, was also for centuries a poor, remote region left to its own devices. One exception has always been the 'white city' of Mérida, the capital of the state of Yucatán, which has a population of more than 1 million. Of these, more than half have a Mayan heritage, and their language and way of life still predominate in the city and surrounding countryside. Mérida has also conserved much of its colonial splendour in the *centro histórico,* while avenues of fine mansions reflect the fact that for years at the start of the 20th century it was reputed to have more millionaires than any other city in the world. This was thanks to the fortunes made from sisal rope-making from the henequen plants grown around the city, although this wealth went hand-in-hand with lives of grinding poverty for the Mayan workers on the plantations. Nowadays, Mérida owes its wealth mainly to the tourists who come to visit the nearby Mayan remains at sites such as Chichén Itza, Uxmal, or Palenque.

The Caribbean side of the Yucatán peninsula is occupied by the state of Quintana Roo. This is the most recent state of the 32 in the Mexican union, officially recognized as recently as 1974. It is also the most easterly state, bordering the Caribbean Sea and sharing a frontier with Belize in the south. Since the 1970s, with the development of Cancún as a mega tourist centre (the city has become a playground of choice for hundreds of thousands of US students on their 'spring break') and the creation of the so-called Riviera Maya, Quintana Roo has been transformed from a slow, relaxed corner of Mexico to a region of mass foreign tourism. Archaeological sites such as Chichén Itza are now surrounded with hotels and hostels, with the hot climate attracting visitors all the year round. As elsewhere, this influx has brought problems that have threatened its unique eco-systems, and these are likely to be made worse if and when AMLO's ambitious plan for the Tren Maya (Mayan Train) is completed.

Mexico's southern border runs through the states of Quintana Roo, Tabasco, and Chiapas. It is here at the town of Tecún Umán that trucks cross the bridge into Mexico from Guatemala, while nearby, desperate Central Americans try to get across the River Suchiate by any means they can. Until recently, the Mexican authorities tolerated this influx, but in 2019 as part of the renegotiation of the North American Free Trade Agreement, the incoming Mexican president Andrés Manuel López Obrador yielded to US President Trump's demand he take responsibility for turning back these migrants. AMLO began to deploy thousands of the newly created National Guard to patrol the southern border more aggressively. This led to desperate Central American migrants joining together to create 'caravans' of thousands of men, women, and children determined to force their way through, creating standoffs and confrontation rather than a long-term solution to the problem.

Porfiriato modernization: Main Post Office building in Mexico City (Nick Caistor)

3 History

Mexico derives its name from the Mexica people, also known as the Aztecs. It was their conquest by Spanish adventurers early in the 16th century and the creation of the Spanish colonial capital on the ruins of the Aztec Tenochtitlán that marked the dawn of modern Mexico.

But the history of the territories now occupied by a single nation goes back thousands of years. Mexico has a wealth of ancient cultures and recorded history comparable to that of China or Egypt. It is generally accepted that the first people to settle in the region were nomadic groups who came from Asia across the Bering Straits during the last Ice Age. Gradually the newcomers spread across a vast territory, including what are now the countries of Central America, to people an area known as Mesoamerica. Agriculture began with the cultivation of maize, squash, beans, chillies, and cotton. The Popol Vuh, the creation account of the Quiché Mayans, shows how important maize was to all these cultures. The gods are said to have first made human beings out of mud, but they dissolved. The next figures were made of wood, but the gods did not like them, and destroyed them. Finally the ancestors of the Quiché people were fashioned from ground maize, and thrived.

The Olmecs and other early cultures

The earliest properly identifiable Mesoamerican culture was that of the Olmecs, who lived from between 1500 and 400 BC on the Caribbean coast, in what today are the states of Tabasco and Veracruz. La Venta, built on a river island close to the Gulf of Mexico, and dating from more than 2,500 years ago is the most impressive Olmec site, offering tantalizing clues as to their way of life. As with all the early peoples, the Olmecs constructed huge ceremonial pyramids: the main one at La Venta, built of many superimposed layers of clay because there was little available stone in the region, stands more than 30 metres high and is 128 metres in diameter. It is at the centre of an impressive group of ceremonial buildings, whose exact purpose has not yet been accurately defined. Beyond these remains, and the typical enigmatic giant helmeted heads buried in the ground here and at a similar site at San Lorenzo, little is known of Olmec beliefs or daily life.

In central Mexico, the most important ancient centre was the city of Teotihuacán, some 40 kilometres north-east of what is now Mexico City. More than 2,000 years ago, Teotihuacán (the Place of the Gods) is thought to have had some 20,000 inhabitants, living in a well-ordered metropolis with residential areas, artisan workshops, a market, and a magnificent ceremonial centre, dedicated in the main to the rain god Tlaloc. Massive pyramids and temples line the central Avenue of the Dead, with the temple to the plumed serpent Quetzalcoatl being the most spectacular, together with pyramids of the Sun and Moon. After dominating the surrounding region for several centuries, the city of Teotihuacán appears to have been abandoned at some point in the 8th century. There is much debate about the reasons for this sudden collapse: was it due to over-population, a devastating fire, an earthquake, or some other natural disaster?

Rivalling the splendour of Teotihuacán were the Mayans. They flourished on the Yucatán peninsula, in northern Guatemala, Belize, and Honduras between AD 300 and AD 900, and nowadays the remains of their cities and temples at places such as Chichén Itza, Palenque, and Uxmal attract thousands of visitors every year.

The Mayan pyramids, temples, ball game courts, stellar observatories as well as sculptures and hieroglyphics reveal an astonishing level of development. The Mayans evolved a complex calendar, are said to have used the concept of zero, and traded extensively in jade and other precious stones with other parts of Mesoamerica. But as with the residents of Teotihuacán, the size of their population seems to have led to their dispersion and downfall, with a drought, deforestation, or other ecological disaster making their elaborate city-states unsustainable.

The Yucatán peninsula has more than 40 of these ancient sites. All of them have elaborately engraved *stelae* depicting their gods or rulers, with hieroglyphics providing dates and historical details. The enduring presence of their life and culture is evidenced by the 2 million people of Mayan heritage living in the southern states of Mexico and northern Guatemala, keeping alive their languages and some of their traditions.

Also in the south of today's Mexico, in the state of Oaxaca, the city of Monte Albán (White Mountain) was another hub of a civilization, thought to have thrived from 500 BC to AD 500. Sculptures, pottery, and writing from this centre of the Zapotec world show considerable sophistication and grace, particularly in the *stelae* known as the Dancers, showing elaborately twisted human forms. While Monte Albán was the administrative centre of the ancient Zapotecs, nearby Mitla was their most important religious complex, and was still in use when the Spaniards arrived in the early 16th century.

Chacmool and Quetzalcoatl

In the central regions of Mexico, the most prominent people before the arrival of the Mexica were the Toltecs. They settled around Tula in today's state of Hidalgo (north of Mexico City) some time in the 10th century AD. For the first time, there are written records that give them not only a distinct identity, but also a named historical leader, Mixcóatl. These were a warrior people, who appear to have lived by exacting tribute from surrounding groups.

The typical Chacmool reclining statues found in their ceremonial centres have stone bowls on their stomachs, said to be where the blood of their captured victims was poured to appease the gods, in particular the plumed serpent Quetzalcoatl. Toltec architectural remains also boast numerous monumental caryatids or Atlante figures used to hold up the wooden beams of their large ceremonial buildings.

The arrival of the Mexica

The Toltecs were venerated by the Mexica or Aztecs, who were relative latecomers to the Valley of Mexico. Originally a nomadic group living in the deserts in the northern deserts, they migrated south in the 13th century and settled on the fertile lands around Lake Texcoco. It was on an island in this lake that in 1325 they founded their capital Tenochtitlán, at a point where, legend has it, they saw an eagle eating a snake. This discovery is still commemorated on the national flag of Mexico, with the central panel showing an eagle perched on a prickly pear plant triumphantly holding the snake in its mouth.

The Aztecs were well-organized and tough fighters, and gradually subdued the other indigenous groups in the valley, often taking the defeated warriors for human sacrifice. Their fifth ruler, Moctezuma I, is seen as the founder of the Aztec empire in the mid-1400s: his rule extended as far away as Veracruz in the east and Oaxaca to the south. At the turn of the 16th century, Aztec power was at its height, with their capital Tenochtitlán containing perhaps as many as 200,000 people, and trade with regions beyond the Valley of Mexico bringing in gold, silver, jade, and other precious goods.

But the Aztec empire was fragile, and Moctezuma II was to see its complete downfall. This was due in part to an Aztec myth, according to which a fair-haired god Quetzalcoatl would appear for a second time from the east, and bring an end to the world as the Aztecs knew it.

An Aztec calendar stone (Nick Caistor)

Spanish conquest

Spanish explorers had reached the Mexican mainland in Yucatán and Tabasco in 1517 and 1518, but had not advanced far inland. In the following year, 1519, Hernán Cortes and his 500 men landed on the eastern coast of Mexico and founded the settlement of Villa Rica de la Vera Cruz (close to what is now the site of Mexico's only nuclear plant at Laguna Verde). Cortés had heard of the fabulous riches of the Aztec empire and its capital Tenochtitlán, and soon headed for the city. Along the way he gathered allies among the local peoples, many of whom were angry at the tributes they were forced to pay to the Mexica. He was also helped by an indigenous interpreter called Malinalli, better known as La Malinche. She gave birth to a son by Cortés, baptized with the Christian name of Martín, and so is regarded

Cortés and Malinche, from the Lienzo de Tlaxcala held at the British Museum (Nick Caistor)

as the founder of the mixed race that typifies Mexico since the Spanish conquest.

The story of the overthrow of the Aztec stronghold has been told and retold thousands of times, including by members of the Cortés's invading army. As so often, we have only the victors' account of what happened. Initially received ceremoniously by the Aztec emperor Moctezuma II, the Spaniards were at first dazzled by the riches and majestic temples of Tenochtitlán, comparing its splendour to that of Venice. However, Cortés and his commanders grew increasingly nervous at their precarious position surrounded by thousands of potentially hostile warriors, and soon took Moctezuma prisoner. He was still allowed to rule his people, but Cortés was determined to rule him. It was not long before Moctezuma II met a violent death: the Spaniards insisted that it was his own people who had killed him, while indigenous versions put the blame on the invaders.

After his death, he was replaced by a new young emperor, Cuauhtémoc (Falling Eagle). His followers began to harass the Spanish troops, who were forced to abandon the city on what became known ever afterwards as the *Noche triste* (Sad Night). Eventually, Cortés managed to regroup his forces, and by mid-1521 had retaken Tenochtitlán, although, as one of their chroniclers put it: 'in order to win the city, it was necessary to demolish it.'

New Spain

Cortés at once began to build his own city right on top of the Aztec one. A cathedral was begun next to what had been the main Aztec temple, and Cortés himself took over several palaces in the centre and in Coyoacán to the south of the city. Many of his commanders were rewarded with huge estates or *haciendas*, on which the indigenous locals were used as slave labour. What the Spaniards proudly called New Spain was by far its biggest colony in the Americas, eventually stretching from what is now the state of Oregon in the United States in the north down to Panama in the Central American isthmus.

Cortés was unable to enjoy his hard-won wealth and prestige for long. By 1528 the Spanish crown sought to rein him and his fellow conquistadores in. He was sent back to Spain to face charges of abuse of power in office. A viceroy was appointed instead to ensure that Emperor Carlos V's wishes were carried out in the new colony. Cortés was eventually cleared of the charges against him, and returned to New Spain, but was unable to regain his former power, and eventually went back to Seville, where he died in 1547.

Under the viceroys, a pyramid structure was created that was to last for three centuries. At the top of the pyramid were the *peninsulares* or people born in Spain. They often owned extensive lands, and occupied the most important positions in the colonial administration. Then came the *criollos* or people of Spanish descent born in Mexico; below them in terms of power and influence were the increasing number of mixed race *mestizos*. At the bottom were several million indigenous people, as well as perhaps 200,000 black slaves imported to work on sugar plantations, or as domestic servants.

The Sword and the Cross

The Spanish conquest of Latin America has been labelled as that of the 'sword and the cross', and the introduction of Christianity brought more huge changes to Mexico. An attempt to prove that the Christian God was also present in these new lands was at the root of the legend of the Virgin of Guadalupe, the patron saint of Mexico. Juan Diego, an indigenous peasant, was said to have had a vision of the Virgin Mary on the hilltop of Tepeyac, north of Mexico City, previously a place of worship to the Aztec earth goddess. This dark-skinned virgin soon became the spiritual mother of the creoles and many of the indigenous groups, in a melding of earlier beliefs with Christianity that is still prevalent today, especially in the south of the country.

As with all its colonies, Spain allowed only trade with the mother country. Manufactured goods were all imported, and Mexico's mineral and agricultural riches were sent back to the peninsula. Gradually over the 17th and 18th centuries, as Mexico's population and wealth grew and Spain's grip on the vast colony loosened, a vigorous and distinctive society grew up in Mexico. Universities were opened, books printed, and trade increased with other parts of Latin America and the Spanish colonies across the Pacific in the Philippines. As the number of those born in Mexico grew to over 7 or 8 million, with only perhaps 25,000 *peninsulares* attempting to control the whole system, social and political unrest began to develop.

¡Viva Mexico!

At the end of the 18th century and early in the 19th, encouraged by the ideals of the French revolution and the collapse of the Habsburg dynasty in Spain, sporadic rebellions against colonial rule broke out in Mexico City and in several regions of Mexico. Most famously, the priest Manuel Hidalgo led a revolt in the provincial city of Guanajuato. On 16 September 1810 in the town of Dolores, he launched the cry of 'Viva Mexico! Long live our Lady of Guadalupe! Death to bad government! Death to the *gachupines* (the Spaniards)!' He soon gathered a peasant army of some 50,000 around him, and won several battles against loyalist forces as he advanced towards Mexico City. Then, in a move that is still the subject of fierce debate, he decided not to push on and take the capital, but instead withdrew to Guadalajara, more than 400 kilometres away. Before long, loyalist troops had regrouped and defeated his irregular forces; Hidalgo was captured, tortured by the Inquisition to confess his sins, and executed by firing squad.

Hidalgo's example led to outbreaks of rebellion throughout Mexico. Soon another priest, José María Morelos, became leader of the revolt against Spanish rule. He was so successful that in November 1814 he issued a Solemn Declaration of Independence and founded what he called the Kingdom of Anáhuac. The constitution of this new nation called for the separation of powers between executive, legislative, and judiciary, the establishment of an elected assembly, an end to slavery, and equality of all races before the law. However, Morelos was also soon hunted down, captured and shot, and his attempt to free Mexico from Spanish rule ended in failure.

Rebel groups continued the struggle for the next six years, confronted by the *peninsulares* and well-trained royalist troops under the command of the young Agustín de Iturbide. He soon enjoyed such a dominant position that by 1821 he succeeded in bringing both the rebels and those still loyal to the Spanish crown together to promulgate what became known as the Plan of Iguala. This called for independence from Spain, but had little of the revolutionary fervour of Hidalgo and Morelos' earlier proclamations. On 28 September 1821, Iturbide sat in the viceregal chair in Mexico City's cathedral and signed the 'Act of Independence of the Mexican Empire.'

Kicking out the *gachupines* (most were forced to leave by 1825) did not lead to stable government. Over the next decades, Mexico lost half its territory; faced invasion by the United States and France; was twice an empire; had 50 governments; and was several times a dictatorship. The vast majority of Mexicans continued to live in the countryside, working as *peones* on the large estates, in the mines, or as peasant farmers with little land of their own.

Within a few months of the 1821 declaration of independence, hopes of a more democratic system were dashed when Iturbide had himself proclaimed emperor. His rule was short-lived: in 1823 he was deposed by the army, led by Antonio López de Santa Anna, and went into exile in Italy and then England. When Iturbide tried to make a return to Mexico, he was captured and publicly executed, watched by the same crowds who only a few years before had hailed him as their emperor.

Santa Anna

It was only then that a new national constitution was passed, and Mexico finally declared a republic. Much of the next three decades was dominated politically by one man: General Antonio Santa Anna, who held power no fewer than eleven times. Elected president for the first time in 1833, he soon dismissed Congress and proclaimed himself supreme dictator. In 1836 he led his troops into Texas against Texans wanting to be free of rule by Mexico, and wiped out the garrison at the famous battle of the Alamo. Retribution was swift, and defeat on the battlefield also led to Santa Anna being ousted from power back in Mexico.

However, only two years later, Santa Anna was again at the head of an army trying to repel other foreign forces, this time the French, who had sent a punitive force to Veracruz. Although defeated, Santa Anna was regarded as a national hero, and once more elected president.

A few years later, the United States annexed Texas, and Santa Anna again declared war, with disastrous results. By September 1847 triumphant US troops had entered Mexico City, and Santa Anna was forced to accept the terms of the Guadalupe Hidalgo treaty, which ceded 780,000 square miles of Mexican territory to the United States, including Texas, California and other US western states.

The Reform Movement

Back in power yet again in 1853, Santa Anna now styled himself the 'Most Serene Highness', but once more he ruled only briefly. Voices in many parts of Mexico began calling for sweeping political reforms to put an end to his autocratic rule. In 1855, the reformers issued the Ayutla Plan, which called for a federal, secular state of Mexico. The country was increasingly divided between a conservative faction, supported by the big land-owners and the Catholic Church, and the liberal reformers who were pressing for greater democracy. The struggle between the two sides lasted for several years, but in 1857 a new constitution was finally passed, separating church and state, abolishing slavery, and establishing a representative republican democracy. However, this was not the end of the conflict, and it took another three years of civil strife until Benito Juárez became president in January 1861. A lawyer and politician, Juárez came from a poor Zapotec family from Oaxaca, and was the first president of indigenous origin.

Juárez inherited a country that had been made bankrupt by the years of fighting and weak government. In July 1861 he declared that Mexico was bankrupt and therefore could not pay off any of its huge foreign debt for at least two years. So began one of the strangest interludes in the history of 19th-century Mexico. France was one of the main debtor nations, and its emperor Napoleon III sent an expeditionary force to Mexico to recover the debt and oust Juárez.

With the active support of the conservative groups in Mexico, French troops occupied Mexico City, as US forces had done less than 20 years earlier. Napoleon III, seeing the opportunity to counteract US influence in the Americas, then hit on the idea of sending the unfortunate Habsburg Archduke Maximilian to become Mexico's second modern-day emperor. At first Maximilian and his wife Carlota were welcomed enthusiastically by ordinary Mexicans, and set about converting Mexico City into a replica of their fiefdoms in Europe. However, Napoleon III soon found it necessary to withdraw his troops to face the rising threat from Prussia, and Maximilian and his conservative supporters proved no match for Juárez's stubborn guerrilla fighters, backed from the south of Mexico by the young Porfirio Díaz. The hapless emperor was captured trying to defend Querétaro, and shot by firing squad in 1867. His corpse was hastily buried, with a pair of black glass eyes taken from a statue of the Virgin replacing his own shattered ones. Carlota returned to her native Belgium, where she lived half-mad in a remote castle until 1927.

The Porfiriato

Benito Juárez returned in triumph to rule Mexico, and in 1871 became the first elected president to complete his period in office. Further liberal reforms were curtailed due to his sudden death a year later, which again led to several years of unrest in the country. Eventually, a former military colleague who had fought under Juárez against the French came to the fore, but he was to take Mexico in a very different direction.

This man was José de la Cruz Porfirio Díaz Mori, and his 35-year rule known as the Porfiriato brought profound changes to Mexico and all Mexicans. His slogan of *'poca política, mucha administración'* (little politics, a lot of administration) saw him bring in a team of *científicos* (the technocrats of today) to apply 'scientific' rules to the development of the country. At the same time he made sure, often by ruthless means, that there was little political debate or opposition. Porfirio Díaz opened up Mexico to foreign capital, with investments that modernized mining and agriculture, saw the expansion of ports and exports, and promoted the construction of railways and the development of industry. Some 20,000 kilometres of lines linking the capital with the north and the Gulf of Mexico were built during his decades in power.

This modernization and opening to the outside world came at a high price for many poorer Mexicans. With the industrialization of agriculture and the cultivation of cash crops such as tobacco, sugar, and coffee, landholdings were increasingly concentrated in the hands of the big estate owners. As many as a quarter of a million peasant farmers were forced off the land and flooded to the cities, creating areas of poverty and misery in the slums of Mexico City, Monterrey, and elsewhere.

Porfirio Díaz was re-elected president no fewer than seven times. He undermined the power of the legislative and the judiciary, and periodically clamped down on any independent press. By the turn of the 20th century, however, opposition to the ageing dictator was growing, not only among the liberal urban middle classes and some organized workers, but in many regions of the countryside.

Revolt and revolution

The first serious political threat to Porfirio's regime came in the 1910 elections, when Francisco I. Madero, a liberal politician who had spent years in exile in the United States, emerged as a serious rival. Porfirio had him locked up, declared himself the victor at the polls, and proudly celebrated the centenary of independence from Spain (the Angel of Independence in Mexico City being perhaps the most celebrated centennial monument). Díaz and his followers had gravely underestimated the threat from Madero and others pushing for democratic reforms; within a year he was on his way into exile in Paris, and the first act of what became known as the Mexican Revolution had begun.

The stirrings of revolt came from the countryside in the north and in the central state of Morelos, where the owners of large-scale sugar plantations evicted many peasant farmers from their lands. Madero, who had escaped from jail and fled to the United States, returned, assembled a rebel army, and took the strategic border city of Ciudad Juárez. Threatened by this military

19th-century slums (US Library of Congress)

insurgency, Porfirio Díaz agreed to step down, and in June 1911 Madero entered Mexico City in triumph. Fresh elections were called, and in November 1911 he took over as president.

President Madero was immediately faced by challenges from left and right. The conservatives wanted little to change under an elected government, and wished him basically to continue the previous regime. The left, especially revolutionary leaders such as Emiliano Zapata in Morelos, wanted Madero to bring in far more radical reforms, particularly with regard to land ownership. Madero used the federal army to keep both sides in check, but made the fatal mistake of appointing General Victoriano Huerta as commander-in-chief. Huerta proved disloyal, and over 10 days in February 1913 his troops attacked government forces and supporters in the heart of the capital, in what became known as the 'decena trágica'. Madero was captured, imprisoned, and then shot when allegedly trying to escape.

Huerta then used the army to impose anti-democratic rule, dismissing elected state governors and other officials and replacing them with army officers. But Huerta, lacking political skill, relied on repression to keep the country quiet. It was not long before fresh rebellions broke out in the north and elsewhere. Another general, Venustiano Carranza, called for a return to constitutional rule, and became the head of the 'constitutionalist' forces. In 1914, his army, together with those of regional caudillos such as Pancho Villa in the north and Zapata to the south, took on Huerta's army. Villa, born Doroteo Arango, was a poor peasant from the northern state of Chihuahua who started out as a bandit but became a charismatic popular military leader dedicated to the cause of the revolution. In April 1914, Villa's División del Norte successfully took the key city of Torreón, and Huerta's days were numbered. As Porfirio Díaz had done before him, he boarded a ship for exile.

Carranza was anxious not to repeat the mistakes of the moderate Madero. 'A revolution which compromises is not a revolution', was one of his slogans, and he purged the army and officials who had served under Huerta, bringing in a new generation of revolutionary sympathisers. A host of laws and decrees sought to strip the big land owners of their lands; the right for workers to organize in unions was recognized; a minimum wage established; and the peons who worked as virtual slaves in the vast southern estates were enfranchized. The federal army was disbanded.

The different factions found it impossible to reach any political compromise. There was no dominant ideology, as in the Russian revolution; the supporters of the Constitutionalists under Carranza and his loyal general Alvaro Obregón, Villa and his followers, Zapata, and other regional leaders, all pulled in different directions. In 1914–1915 a third round of armed conflict broke out, in what became known as the 'war of the victors'. In late 1914 Villa and Zapata and their followers entered Mexico City, forcing General Obregón to retreat to the east. But the power of these two revolutionary leaders was largely based on their home regions, whereas Carranza exercised control from the centre, and his loyal General Obregón proved to be a far more effective military leader than Villa, while Zapata had by now withdrawn to his Morelos stronghold.

With the defeat of Villa in the north, Carranza gradually won the day. By early 1917 he was able to call a constituent assembly that eventually agreed a new national constitution and widespread agrarian reform. This built on the liberal reforms of the great 1857 charter, additionally barring the Catholic Church from politics and from primary education, while ushering in sweeping land reform and bolstering workers' rights. Carranza was elected as the first president under this new constitution, and

General Carranza and loyalist officers (Nick Caistor)

ruled for three years in a Mexico gradually emerging from the social turmoil that had seen half a million people killed, many more uprooted from their homes and livelihoods, and violence installed as a way of life.

However, as with his immediate predecessors, Carranza did not live to enjoy his position for long. When he tried to impose his own choice as candidate for the 1920 presidential election, he was chased out of office by Obregón and his supporters. Carranza fled on a train to the port of Veracruz, but died in murky circumstances before he got there.

4 The revolution made government

General Obregón inherited a country weary of war. The two popular leaders of the revolution were no longer on the scene: Zapata had been betrayed and killed in 1919, and Pancho Villa was assassinated in 1923.

During his term as president from 1920 to 1924, Obregón set about reconstructing the state and introducing reforms in many areas, as did his successor Plutarco Calles (1924–1928). They gradually managed to assert civilian control of the army, successfully putting down revolts in 1923 and 1928. But there were still challenges to the new regime: in 1928 Obregón was elected for a second term, but was shot and killed in a Mexico City restaurant

Zapata (US Library of Congress)

by a fervent Catholic, angry at the government's anti-clerical policies.

The 1917 constitution had made primary education secular, kept Catholic priests out of politics, and banned public religious festivals, including popular fiestas and pilgrimages. During his first presidency, Calles reinforced this anti-Catholic drive, bringing in a law that required all priests to register with the state.

The Cristero War

The Catholic Church's response was to stop providing Mass, and soon there was rebellion against the government by Catholics in many regions of the country. What was known as the Cristiada or Cristero War became the greatest challenge to political stability in the second half of the 1920s. Calles managed to stifle the rebellion, in which more than 70,000 people are said to have died, and set about further strengthening the power of the central state. At the same time, he continued to promote secular public education; the number of primary schools grew by a third in the 1920s, while literacy rates also grew steadily.

The most important move in the consolidation of the post-revolution regime was the 1929 establishment of the Partido Nacional Revolucionario (PNR, the National Revolutionary Party), which after several mutations in 1946 became the PRI.

The PNR brought together the many different pro-government parties and organized labour and peasant organizations that had emerged after the revolution. The labour movement was concentrated in a national grouping, the CROM (Confederación Regional Obrera Mexicana, the Mexican Regional Workers' Confederation). Presidents Obregón and Calles relied on the CROM's support for their centralizing efforts, and in return gave the organization a crucial role in labour reform, the push for better wages and conditions, and collective bargaining.

Calles also stepped up the expropriation (*reparto*) of many big estates, with land being given over to *ejidos*. These peasant collectives could now work the land for their own benefit, although ownership remained with the state. This tied the peasant farmers, who still made up two thirds of Mexicans, more closely to the growing central state, while guaranteeing the land could not be bought by rich landlords.

The revolutionary nationalism embodied by the PNR, even though it was not a well-defined ideology like that of the Marxist-Leninists of the Russian revolution, had an equally profound effect on the whole of Mexican society for the rest of the 20th century – and, as Mexicans proudly point out, it lasted longer (just) than its Soviet counterpart.

Lázaro Cárdenas

Even after his presidential term finished in 1928, Calles, known as the *jefe màximo*, continued to be the dominant figure in Mexican politics at the start of the 1930s. Calles thought this could continue when he sponsored a young revolutionary leader Lázaro Cárdenas as his choice for the next president. But he misjudged his man, and soon after Cárdenas duly won office in 1934, he sent Calles packing into exile, like so many of his predecessors.

It was under Cárdenas' rule from 1934 to 1940 that the new state emerging from the revolution took definitive shape. Cárdenas himself travelled incessantly throughout Mexico in his 'green train', supervising the handover of big estates to *ejidos*. A total of some 19 million hectares of land was redistributed during his presidency, half as much again as the total achieved by previous administrations, thus cementing his support in the countryside.

As the Mexican economy revived after the Great Depression, a new national labour organization, the CTM (Confederación de Trabajadores Mexicanos), came to the fore. The CTM fought effectively for workers' rights, collective bargaining, and 'closed shops' that gave the union tremendous power. In return, they backed Cárdenas and his radical agenda.

Cárdenas nationalized many industries, including the railway system in 1937. But he is best known for his 1938 expropriation of the dozen or so foreign oil companies operating in Mexico. Their companies were transformed into the state-owned PEMEX (Petróleos Mexicános), the first nationalized oil firm in the developing world. This move sealed Cárdenas's popularity and helped cement support behind the dominant official party, which in the same year he renamed as the Partido de la Revolución Mexicana, (the PRM or Party of the Mexican Revolution).

Cárdenas also took a strongly independent line in foreign affairs, welcoming more than 30,000 refugees from the Spanish Civil War and refusing to recognize Franco. This stance continued for many years, with Mexico adopting a supportive attitude towards revolutions in Cuba and Central America, and continuing to welcome exiles from Latin American dictatorships (including both the Cuban Fidel Castro and the Argentinian Ernesto 'Che' Guevara). By the 1970s, this foreign policy came to seem increasingly at odds with the PRI's domestic policies.

Dedocracia

By now the system known as *dedocracia*, whereby the incumbent president personally 'pointed to' his successor from the same official party, was well established, thus ensuring stability and continuity for the next *sexenio*, or six-year presidential term. So it was that in 1940 Cárdenas's chosen successor Manuel Avila Camacho was elected. During the Second World War, he patched up relations with the United States. Thousands of Mexicans living in the USA volunteered to fight, while many thousands more went there to work in agriculture under the *bracero* programme that was to last until the 1960s. Mexico eventually joined up on the side of the allies on 1 June 1942. The Mexican air squadron the Aztec Eagles took part in the final assault on Japan.

President Camacho used the boost the conflict gave to Mexico's exports to promote national industry, and to strengthen the state. In 1943 his government set up the Mexican Secretariat of Health and Assistance, creating a public health system, and the Mexican Social Security Institute, establishing state pensions. At the same time, Camacho rowed back on any further land reform, and curbed the CTM's power.

Camacho's successor, Miguel Alemán (1946–1952), was able to use Mexico's buoyant economic position after the war to boost infrastructure and improve living standards for the growing middle class. His most famous slogan was that he wanted every Mexican to be able to enjoy a 'Cadillac, a cigar and a ticket to the bullfight'.

Post-war boom: the Viaducto Alemán in the capital (Nick Caistor)

Alemán was also the president who in 1946 gave the official party its current name of the PRI, the Institutional Revolutionary Party. By now it was indeed an institution, controlling all levels of power throughout Mexico, and relying on its dominant position to keep both its rural and working class supporters happy. This brought stable government and continued economic growth that was the envy of many other Latin American countries, often mired in crises with dictators, military rule, and seesawing economic fortunes.

The PRI in power

Fifty years on from the revolution, Mexico was virtually a one-party state. Other political parties such as the PAN (set up in 1939 along Christian-Democratic lines) did exist, but had little hope of winning power except at local level. The system that had evolved into the PRI – what the poet Octavio Paz called the 'philanthropic ogre', gave Mexicans a strong sense of national and personal identity, as the regime stressed it was the direct descendant of the revolution, and the guarantor of its gains.

Increasingly, its policies were closer to the interests of the business elites, and although the state employed a huge proportion of the population either as public servants or in state-owned companies, many ordinary Mexicans felt left out, alienated by the rhetoric and overblown official pride at the regime's achievements. Although the PRI's hegemony was to last another 40 or so years, it was increasingly by means of repression and a stale reliance on revolutionary slogans and rituals that it retained power.

The repressive face of PRI rule was revealed most starkly in the 1968 massacre of 300 or more students in Mexico City a few weeks prior to the Olympic Games. These killings demonstrated to many Mexicans just how far the PRI regime was prepared to go to preserve its image to the outside world. When President Luis Echeverria came to power in 1970, at first it seemed he wanted to promote reconciliation: the leaders of the 1968 student movement who were in exile in Chile were allowed to return, and political prisoners were released. However, he created the feared paramilitary force known as *Los Halcones* (The Hawks) and in 1971 they were involved in another massacre of students known as the Corpus Christi massacre. Echeverria went on to suppress left-wing groups in the early 1970s, and was seen by many as being responsible for permitting widespread torture and other illegal measures by the armed forces and the police.

The PRI regime crumbles

The tipping point came with the 1985 earthquake in Mexico City, in which at least 10,000 people died, and hundreds of thousands were left homeless. The government's painfully slow reaction, and the fact that many of the buildings that collapsed were hospitals and schools built by the state and supposedly quake-proof, showed Mexicans how deep-seated were the corruption and disdain for ordinary people among PRI politicians and local officials.

This disaster led left-wing PRI supporters to finally give up on the party and split off to form the PRD (Democratic Revolutionary Party) under the leadership of Cuauhtémoc Cárdenas, the son of the revolutionary 1930s leader. The fact that Cárdenas was widely thought to have been robbed of victory in the 1988

After the devastating 1985 Mexico City earthquake (Centro de la Imagen)

presidential election (the counting of votes mysteriously broke down for several hours before the PRI's Carlos Salinas de Gortari was declared the winner) only served to further undermine the PRI's authority, and before long led to the loss of its hegemonic position.

Modern-day Aztecs (Valeria Arendar)

5 Society

Race

It is estimated that about 20 million people were living in Mexico when Cortés and his Spanish *conquistadores* landed on the mainland early in the 16th century and set about their conquest in the name of the Spanish emperor. Disease, oppression, and neglect reduced these numbers dramatically over the following centuries; many of these groups were scattered to the harshest parts of the country as large colonial landowners took over the most fertile tracts of land.

Three centuries of Spanish rule led to a widespread intermingling of white European colonists and the indigenous communities. This mixture or *mestizaje* has long been a source of debate in Mexico. Some, like the influential poet Octavio Paz in his book *El Laberinto de la Soledad* (The Labyrinth of Solitude) published in the mid-1950s, see Mexican identity as being the product of a tragic rape, symbolized by La Malinche, the Nahua native woman who served as Cortés's interpreter and mistress. In Paz's view, since the first modern-day Mexicans were born from this forced union, ever since, Mexicans are *hijos de la chingada*, destined always to feel illegitimate, and so condemned to the solitude of his book's title.

This demeaning view was certainly that of the Spanish colonists, who looked down on those who could not claim (often spuriously) that they were 100 per cent European, or at least born of Spanish stock in Mexico. A caste system was put in place, with the *peninsulares* at the top of the colonial society's population pyramid, the *mestizos* with darker skins beneath them, and the indigenous groups (and imported black slaves) at the bottom.

After Mexico won its independence from Spain early in the 19th century, other countries such as the United States, France, and Great Britain tended to regard all Mexicans, whatever their ancestry, as inferior physically and culturally. This gave rise to the caricature of the lazy (probably drunken) Mexican asleep under a cactus, waiting for *mañana*.

Mexican identity

It was one of the achievements of the early 20th-century revolution in Mexico to open up an intellectual debate about *Lo Mexicano,* what it meant to be Mexican. Thanks to the spirit of revolutionary nationalism, a new pride in pre-Columbian history and native ancestry came to the fore. This culminated in the work of the philosopher and educationalist José Vasconcelos, who in 1925 published his *La raza cósmica,* with its famous description of Mexicans as the *raza de bronce,* the 'bronze race', forged out of struggle rather than submission to a foreign conqueror, and destined to play a prominent role in the future of the universe.

This new-found pride in *mestizaje* was seized upon by the ruling party that eventually became the PRI to demonstrate they were the upholders of this dual national character. As recently as 1970, President Luis Echeverría could claim: 'We are a *mestizo* people with a *mestizo* culture. We are proud of the two great sources of our national identity.' However, at the same time he added a caveat that was obvious, although it went largely unheeded by his own party: 'backwardness and marginalization in some indigenous groups is the product of underdevelopment. So long as we do not incorporate them into the progress of the whole community, they will be strangers in their own land.'

Indigenous women in Oaxaca (Elva Narcia)

The EZLN uprising

Despite warnings of this kind, the situation of Mexico's indigenous peoples only worsened with the economic crises of the 1980s and 1990s. The tensions created by this centuries-old inequality were made dramatically evident with the January 1994 EZLN (Ejército Zapatista de Liberación Nacional) uprising in Chiapas. The EZLN were demanding greater respect for indigenous cultural and ethnic rights, including a reversal of the decision to end the *ejido* system that emerged out of the 1910 revolution, which had meant indigenous and peasant communities could live and work on land collectively, with no individual owning it.

After violent conflict with the national army that caused hundreds of deaths, there was an uneasy truce between the two sides until a peace accord between the Mexican government and the EZLN was signed at San Andrés Larráinzar in Chiapas in February 1996. As a result of this, in 2001 the national constitution was amended to accommodate some of the indigenous peoples' grievances. These changes were meant to include the right of indigenous communities to self-regulation and autonomy; the preservation of cultural and linguistic identity; and communal property rights.

These were in great part no more than paper promises. Eventually the Zapatistas and other indigenous groups rejected the changes, and refused to take part in any further dialogue with the federal government. In Chiapas, they have formed autonomous municipalities and *caracoles*, communities where they have direct control over local affairs and economic and political decisions.

Indigenous life today

Throughout Mexico, indigenous groups still suffer most from poverty and discrimination. In the 21st century, Mexico's indigenous population makes up approximately 15 per cent of the total. Between them they speak some 60 indigenous languages (although Spanish is Mexico's only official language). The indigenous groups live mostly in the southern states, with more than a million native language speakers in both Oaxaca and Chiapas. A further 2 million Zapotec speakers live in central regions, and there are other concentrations in the mountainous and semi-desert northern region.

Many of these indigenous groups continue with the centuries-old cultivation of basic food crops of maize, squash, and beans in smallholdings. Often nowadays their villages are peopled by women, children, and old men: the younger males have left for the United States either to find seasonal work in the fields of California, Texas, and other southern US states, or to try to achieve more permanent status there. They return to their home villages only for fiestas or to marry, before setting off again. Many other young indigenous men and women head for Mexico's big cities, where they find low-paid manual work and swell the sprawling shanty towns that encircle the capital and other major urban centres.

Migrants

It is not only indigenous people who try to migrate north to the United States. Many thousands of poor Mexicans cross the border without legal documents to earn higher wages and avoid the violence that has grown so tragically in Mexico over recent years. Their remittances are second only to oil and gas exports in terms of foreign currency earnings for Mexico. Successive US administrations have tried to stem this flow, criminalizing and deporting the migrants. This process accelerated in recent years, despite the fact that since the 2008–2009 economic crisis, there has been a net outflow of Mexican-born workers from their northern neighbour. In 2012, President Obama tightened up legislation on undocumented immigrants; an annual average of some 380,000 Mexican immigrants were sent back to their own country between 2009 and 2016.

With the arrival of President Donald Trump to the White House in 2016 this migrant question became a still greater crisis. One of his most strident slogans during the election campaign was his desire to 'build a wall' along the 3,000 kilometre border with Mexico – and his insistence that the Mexicans were going to pay for it. Many of his comments were violently racist: 'When Mexico sends its people, they're not sending their best', he said at one point on the campaign trail. 'They're sending people that have lots of problems, and they're bringing those problems with us [sic]. They're bringing drugs. They're bringing crime. They're rapists. And some, I assume, are good people.' He immediately increased border patrols and speeded up the deportation process, but work on the wall has been piecemeal, is far from complete, and has been funded by the US government.

Young indigenous women meanwhile frequently end up doing poorly paid domestic work for Mexican middle-class urban families. There are said to be a quarter of a million domestic workers in Mexico City alone, the vast majority of them originally speaking a language other than Spanish, and possibly more than 2 million in the country as a whole.

Unacknowledged racism

The lack of basic rights and discrimination suffered by indigenous Mexicans is part and parcel of the largely unacknowledged racism in Mexican society today. The convenient idea of *mestizaje* disguises the fact that the whiter the skin, the greater the chances of better educational and employment opportunities. TV programmes and advertising, styles of dress, tastes in music, and of course the ever-present comparisons with the 'American Dream' offered by the United States all tend to reinforce this prejudice. Domestic worker Marcelina Bautista summed up this attitude in an interview for *The Guardian* newspaper (10 November 2015): 'I had to put up with insults from people who believed they were better than me because they'd studied more, because they didn't value what I did, because I was poor and indigenous, and they held the power.' The plight of indigenous domestic workers like Marcelina was movingly illustrated in Alfonso Cuarón's Oscar-winning film *Roma*.

To his credit, since becoming president, Andres Manuel López Obrador has brought in legislation to increase the rights of workers like Marcelina, and has raised the legal minimum wage. It is no coincidence that the name of his political party MORENA (Movimiento de Regeneración Nacional), is also the Spanish adjective for a dark-skinned woman, and he enjoys a particularly high level of support among poorer Mexicans and indigenous groups, although not among the Zapatistas and their followers, who criticized him from the start of his campaign.

Religious beliefs

His party's name also links back to the most famous dark-skinned symbol in Mexican history, the Virgin of Guadalupe. Every day, thousands of Catholic pilgrims, many of them on their knees, make their way to the shrine of the Virgin on a hilltop to the north of Mexico City. The legend of the appearance of the Virgin Mary to the indigenous peasant Juan Diego soon after the Spanish conquest was a masterstroke in combining the traditional beliefs of the indigenous population with the Catholic religion that was being brought in and promoted from a far-off continent. Equally eloquent is the fact that the shrine to the Christian virgin is built on the site on Tepeyac hill where the pre-Columbian people worshipped Tonantzín, the earth goddess. As with *mestizaje*, the fusion of these two traditions has produced a distinctively Mexican version of Christianity. There is even a popular saying: *Soy ateo, pero guadalupano* ('I'm an atheist, but I believe in Guadalupe').

Nowadays, more than 80 per cent of Mexicans declare themselves to be Catholic, although a much smaller percentage are practising, especially in urban areas. At the same time, it seems that evangelical Protestant churches are having less of an impact in Mexico than in Central America or Brazil. However, the relationship between the Mexican Catholic church and the Mexican state has frequently been one of conflict. The mid-19th century reforms were chiefly aimed at curbing the power and wealth of the church. The 1910 revolution again aimed to limit its strength and influence, and the 1917 constitution declared Mexico to be a secular state, and for public education to be non-religious. For many years, in fact until 1992 under President Carlos Salinas, the Mexican state and the Vatican had no direct diplomatic relations, while priests, nuns, and other religious groups were not permitted to hold services outside churches, or display any tokens of their religion.

The PRI has always been proud of its secular stance and the strict separation of church and state, especially in education. During the years of PRI dominance, the Mexican Catholic church was regarded as reactionary, opposed to progress in many social areas. This was another aspect of the massive change signalled when Vicente Fox, the leader of the PAN (a nationalist party formed with Catholic support in 1939) became president

in the year 2000. A traditional Catholic, he visited the Virgin of Guadalupe shrine for a blessing on the day of his inauguration (something unthinkable for his PRI predecessors), and appointed several staunch Catholics to key positions in his government.

Since then, the Catholic church in Mexico has suffered from scandals of alleged sexual abuse similar to those uncovered all over the world. It has also been heavily criticized for its apparent tolerance (and possible collusion) with the illegal drug cartels. The church hierarchy has also resisted attempts to legalize abortions, and same-sex marriages, and has been slow to respond to the crisis of thousands of migrants entering Mexico from Central America. Only a few local bishops and priests have adopted a more progressive stance, among them Samuel Ruiz in Chiapas, who helped mediate talks between the government and the Zapatistas.

Education

An important legacy of the 1910 revolution was to take education out of the hands of the church and ensure that the new, secular values of the Mexican state were taught throughout the country. The *maestro rural* was a typical figure in the 1930s: a young man sent out to remote rural areas in states where the central government had until then barely had a presence, to inculcate the republican values fought over in the decade of upheaval. Official education stressed the importance of literacy, equality before the law, and a programme of shared education for everyone.

As with many other areas of life in Mexico, by the 1960s and 1970s this legacy was wearing thin. Not only was there huge unrest among university and secondary students in 1968, but it became increasingly clear that public education, often underfunded, was not equipping the emerging generations for life in a modern society. Since then, Mexico has regularly been bottom in the yearly OECD tables of educational standards in 35 countries. Despite boasting the largest university in the world (the UNAM in Mexico City, with more than 250,000 students) and other top-class universities, and although theoretically education is compulsory for all to the age of 18, many young Mexicans still leave school at 14 or earlier with only minimal education. According to recent official statistics, some 27 per cent of indigenous and children from the poorest families are unable to read or write.

In the closing years of the 20th century, the public education system came increasingly to be seen as bloated and inefficient. Teachers were poorly trained and paid, and their main SNTE union, with more than a million members, was regarded as corrupt, full of doubtful practices such as teachers being able to nominate their own replacements. The SNTE, under its legendary powerful leader Esther Gordillo, controlled the education budget and most staffing matters. In the end it was the PRI's own Enrique Peña Nieto who made educational reform one of the main planks of his presidency. In 2013 he announced sweeping measures aimed at improving standards, curbing the SNTE's power and restrictive practices, and making the Education Ministry responsible for teaching appointments rather than the union. As was to be expected, these reforms were strongly opposed by the SNTE union, even though they had widespread public support.

During his election campaign in 2018, AMLO said he would reverse this reform effort, claiming it was part of his PRI predecessor's 'neo-liberal' policies. Instead he promised to increase spending on education, offer students grants, and bring in free school meals, while supporting a different breakaway teachers' union, the CNTE or Coordinadora Nacional de Trabajadores de la Educación.

Countryside and cities

One of the challenges facing the educational system throughout the 20th and 21st centuries in Mexico has been the constant migration from the countryside to towns and cities. This has often caused lack of continuity in schooling and increased levels of desertion. Nowadays, more than three quarters of Mexico's estimated 129 million people live in urban centres. The largest of these is the capital, Mexico City, with approximately 20 million inhabitants living in or around it in the state of Mexico. With most of the country's industry, government agencies and services located there, the capital still acts as a powerful magnet for the young and for those living in the countryside or the poorer southern states. This predominance of the capital, whose inhabitants are known insultingly as *chilangos* by other Mexicans, has a distorting effect on development in the regions, sucking in government expenditure as well as domestic and foreign investment. Attempts to reverse this trend have often been half-hearted and inconsistent.

Despite this, other large cities such as Guadalajara, the capital of state of Jalisco and an important agricultural and cultural centre, Monterrey, which benefits from its proximity to the United States border and prides itself on being the most technologically advanced city in the country, or Veracruz, the main port on the eastern seaboard, all have strong local identities and traditions.

The role of women

Mexico has changed in the past hundred years from a predominantly poor rural society to a modern, urban one, with more than three quarters of the population now living in urban areas. But it often seems that the role of women in Mexican society has remained unchanged. In the countryside, the mother was the centre of the family, and was seen as providing a home, food, and security, and keeping extended relationships together, often with an absent husband or partner. In the urban context, Mexican women have also usually been called upon to provide a stable home for their spouse and children, to the detriment of any professional and personal development beyond the four walls of the family home.

Machismo is still a strong force in the workplace, with women expected to take a subordinate role, to do as their male bosses tell them, to look pretty and leave politics, serious debates and close friendships to the men folk. A Mexican stereotype is the *casa grande* where a wealthy man has his wife and family, and the *casa chica* for his mistress. This patriarchal attitude has been increasingly challenged by recent generations, when young women in particular have shown they can play leading roles in the professions, the arts, and in politics.

Although Lázaro Cárdenas first proposed suffrage for women in 1937, it was not until 1953 that they were entitled to vote in national elections. Since 2018 when Andrés Manuel López Obrador took office, they have made up more than one third of members of Congress. His first cabinet of ministers included an equal number of women and men. In the same year, MORENA's Claudia Sheinbaum, a scientist who had shared the Nobel Peace Prize for her work with the Intergovernmental Panel on Climate Change, became the first woman to be elected mayor of Mexico City.

In 2020, the question of femicide and domestic violence against women in general returned to the headlines, following the death of a 25-year-old young woman who was dismembered and skinned alive by her partner, and the discovery of the body of a seven-year-old girl who had been kidnapped outside her school, sexually assaulted, then murdered. On 9 March 2020, activists called for a 'day without women' as a protest at the number of murders against women, now more than 10 a day. Female employees from the *maquila* factories along Mexico's northern border joined the protest, as well as thousands of office and transport service workers in the big cities throughout the country. More than 80,000 people marched through the streets of the capital. The protesters were particularly incensed at the lack of interest shown by President López Obrador over the issue, and his dismissal of the march as part of a right-wing plot against him. 'It's a strange thing that conservatives have turned into feminists, and we are now *machistas*', he told reporters. He has also refused to meet the relatives of the thousands of disappeared people who marched on the capital.

The press and TV

One area where women in Mexico have played a vital role in recent years is the media. Many of the country's most prominent and fearless journalists, from Carmen Aristegui to Lydia Cacho and Anabel Hernández, have denounced corruption and the increasing violence in everyday life. During President Pena Nieto's government, Aristegui was forced out by one TV company for reporting on disappearances in the state of Guerrero. Frequently though, the media in Mexico is not so principled. Part of the outrage at murders against women came from the fact that two sensationalist newspapers showed the flayed body of the murdered 25 year old on their front pages. Several of the most widely read newspapers regularly publish pictures from the scene of car crashes, or of other murder victims (the *nota roja*) for their readerships' titillation.

There are also more responsible daily publications, all of them privately owned and theoretically independent from the government and political parties. However, they have often had to rely on income from government advertising contracts, which means their political line can sway according to which party is in power. Another form of control employed in the past by the PRI was the monopoly the state supplier has on the production and distribution of newsprint paper.

The growth of more independent media in the 1980s, with the creation of the dailies *La Jornada* and *Uno Mas Uno* and the weekly magazine *Proceso* was another sign of the PRI's loss of hegemonic control, while the creation of the daily *Reforma* in 1993 brought a new professionalism to reporting, and serious attempts to provide more objective coverage. This effort has continued, with more alternative media initiatives appearing. This is especially true in the area of social media, which have grown immensely in the past few years, especially among young Mexicans.

However, daily newspaper readership can be counted in the hundreds of thousands rather than millions, and is mostly concentrated in the middle classes in the capital and other major cities. There are some strong regional and local publications, which tend to more trusted for reliable news than the two main commercial free-to-air TV networks, the dominant TV Azteca and Televisa. Both these outlets concentrate on popular entertainment, whether in the form of the ever popular (often outrageous) *telenovelas* or soap operas that can bring the country to a halt when they reach a climax, or music and comedy, sports, and many dubbed US programmes. The publicly owned Canal 11 concentrates mostly on culture and documentary information. There are also hundreds of local radio stations, which play a vital role in local and regional news.

Mexico is regarded as one of the most dangerous countries in the world for journalists. More than a hundred have been killed since 2000. Many of these were victims of the drug wars, but others have also been murdered by local politicians or wealthy caudillos unwilling to have their lives put under scrutiny. For the most part, journalists are poorly trained and paid, and often have to work for several outlets. In the days of PRI dominance, they often relied on handouts known as *chayote* from the authorities or local politicians as a reward for positive reports about the government. This, and a tendency to report official statements without questioning them, continues to be common practice across every kind of media.

Shopping mall in Mexico City (Sebastián Machado)

Inequality

Mexican society demonstrates the extremes of inequality typical of most developing countries. There are 12 billionaires who regularly figure on *Forbes* magazine's annual 'rich list', notably Carlos Slim and the Larrea family, which owns huge mining interests. Wealthy Mexicans often possess huge estates in the countryside, but spend most of the year in luxury homes or apartments in neighbourhoods such as Interlomas in Mexico City. These neighbourhoods often lie cheek by jowl with the poorest shanty towns where the inhabitants lack electricity and running water.

Some of these informal barrios have now become cities in their own right, with several million people living in poor conditions, such as Nezahualcóyotl and Ecatepec in the state of Mexico. Many of these slum dwellers make up the 25 per cent of Mexicans who work as and when they can in the informal economy, finding employment as casual labourers, street vendors, or in domestic service.

However, despite the obvious poverty in rural areas and in city slums, it can be argued that most of Mexico is now an urban, middle class society. 'Average' Mexicans can hope to own or rent an apartment or house; they will probably have a car, a television, credit cards, the internet; go shopping in a big commercial centre; enjoy eating out and following many leisure pursuits; religious beliefs will be of lesser importance; and as the three elections in the 21st century have shown, party political loyalty is increasingly volatile.

Thanks to the relative economic stability of the past 25 years, these middle class Mexicans will have hopes that life can get better, if not for them, then at least for their offspring. In part this is due to the fact that the number of children per family has fallen dramatically: in the 1960s the fertility rate was 7.3 per fertile mother; the corresponding figure some 50 years later was a little over two. Infant mortality meanwhile has been reduced from 79 per thousand births in 1970 to 11 per thousand 50 years later. Life expectancy has risen from 56 years for men and 60 for women in 1960 to 74 years for males and 79 for females, according to the latest official figures.

6 Economy

In economic terms, Mexico had a good Second World War. Its mineral wealth, the backbone of the country's exports since Spanish colonial days, was much needed by the Allies, as were its oil and agricultural produce. The *bracero* scheme that saw thousands of Mexican workers employed in the United States created a flow of US dollars sent back as remittances that has been vital to the Mexican economy ever since. At the same time, restrictions on imports of manufactured goods meant that national industry, often controlled by the state, was able to flourish.

The boom years

As a result, for three decades from the 1940s to the 1970s, the Mexican economy achieved an annual growth rate of over 6 per cent. Import tariffs protected Mexican industry, which produced everything from heavy industrial machinery to televisions, refrigerators, and other consumer goods. A growing number of Mexicans began to regard themselves as middle class, although the amount of disposable income they had fluctuated widely. This was a period of massive expansion in the number of state employees, and many millions were dependent on the state for employment or benefits.

This stability began to falter in the 1970s, when the dangers of the one-party system and the six-year presidential term became increasingly evident. It had become a maxim that each president was financially cautious during the first half of his term, and then began spending massively to ensure that his successor (named by him) would be backed at the polls.

This was what happened under President Luis Echeverria from 1970 to 1976. By the end of his period on the Eagle Throne, inflation was rampant (at more than 20 per cent), unemployment was on the increase, and the Mexican peso was under severe strain from the government's foreign debt repayments. All of this led to a 43 per cent devaluation of the national currency early in 1976.

The curse of oil

The next PRI president, José López Portillo, thought the answer to all these economic woes had been magically found when huge oil reserves were discovered in the Cantarell field in the Gulf of Mexico. These discoveries boosted proven oil reserves to more than 72 billion barrels. López Portillo's government began a spending splurge based on borrowing internationally against the potential income from developing the oil fields, and spent much of the funds on ill thought out mega infrastructure projects, and the state takeover of failing businesses. Mexico's foreign debt increased by some US$60 billion.

As with many countries, the oil boom in Mexico proved to be as much a curse as a blessing. In October 1981, with the international oil price falling, the Mexican government was forced to drastically devalue the peso from 20 Mexican pesos to the dollar to 160 pesos/dollar. This dramatically increased the foreign dollar debt, especially to US commercial banks. As economic instability increased, capital flight intensified, putting even more pressure on the Mexican peso.

By August of the following year, Mexico was forced to default on the $80 billion sovereign debt, in the middle of an international debt crisis (as Benito Juárez had done in very different circumstances almost 120 years earlier). The entire Mexican private banking system, together with most people's savings, was nationalized. This time there were no foreign invasions, but the IMF offered a $3.8 billion loan in return for the Mexican government cutting back on spending and opening up the Mexican economy to foreign investment by reducing tariffs and allowing foreign firms to compete with state-owned concerns.

In 1983, with Miguel de la Madrid in the presidency, the Mexican economy shrank by more than 4 per cent, and per capita GDP fell by a similar amount. Inflation ran at an annual rate of 100 per cent for several months, and unemployment reached record levels, especially in the countryside. The crisis lasted until well into the second half of the decade, with low international oil prices and a debt burden amounting to some 78 per cent of annual GDP. In the five years between 1983 and 1988, average economic growth was only an estimated 0.1 per cent.

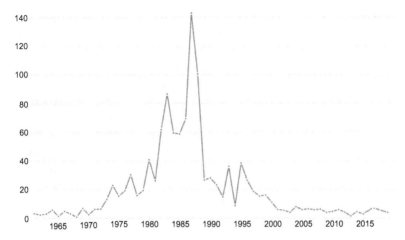

Inflation (%) in Mexico, 1961–2019
Source: World Bank, 2020

Neo-liberalism

These years saw the transformation of the Mexican economy from a corporatist state-controlled model to the free-market, neo-liberal orthodoxy then being promoted by the IMF, the World Bank, and administrations in Washington. Foreign investment regulations were eased to allow investment in all areas of the economy (except the precious oil industry), and Mexican financial markets were opened up. At the end of 1991, the nationalized private banking sector was privatized once more.

All these measures were undertaken by PRI governments, who in their rhetoric still claimed to be pursuing the revolutionary nationalism that had underpinned their successful hold on power for decades. So when the North American Free Trade Agreement came into force in January 1994, President Carlos Salinas de Gortari could boast: 'What we are doing today is carrying out the reform of the revolution that will guarantee its permanence and vitality'.

By this stage, however, almost nobody in Mexico was fooled, and this hollowing out of the PRI's inheritance from the revolution played a big part in its defeat at the 2000 elections. Carlos Salinas himself became a figure of fun, if not disdain: in 1995 there was widespread talk in Mexico of a vampire animal known as the '*chupacabras*' going around sucking the blood of animals and humans. Soon the best-selling doll among street vendors in Mexico City was the balding figure of the president, equipped with Dracula-style fangs.

To many local observers, it had been surprising that the PRI had succeeded in remaining in power for so long. Over the previous five decades, Mexican society had changed enormously. Whereas in the 1940s, more than 60 per cent of the population had lived in the countryside; by the 1990s almost three quarters of Mexicans were living in cities and towns. Increasingly, the new generations wanted the most up-to-date consumer goods, cars, and other products that they could purchase from anywhere, rather than relying on whatever Mexico's national industries could provide.

The big sell-off

President Salinas oversaw the sell-off or closure of 940 state concerns, including everything from the airline Aeromexico (dubbed 'AeroMaybe' because of its unreliable schedules) to major steel works, shipyards, and sugar mills. The sales are calculated to have brought in more than $21 billion. Most of this went towards reducing the country's foreign debt, but at the same time it left almost half a million Mexicans out of work. The process also created a handful of oligarchs who had the necessary wealth to snap up state-owned concerns and become even richer in the process, as was the case in Russia. Perhaps the most contentious

Five Mexican municipalities with greater volume of population in poverty, 2015

State	Municipality	Population	Percentage of poverty (%)	Population in poverty	Contribution to the poverty population of the five municipalities (%)
México	Ecatepec de Morelos	1,840,902	42.7	786,843	24.8
Puebla	Puebla	1,719,828	40.6	699,016	22.0
Distrito Federal	Iztapalapa	1,903,552	35.0	665,408	21.0
Guanajuato	Leon	1,659,125	31.5	522,736	16.5
Baja California	Tijuana	1,693,494	29.5	499,136	15.7
Total		*8,816,901*	*36.0*	*3,173,139*	*100.0*

Source: CONEVAL, 'Rural poverty in Mexico: prevalence and challenges', 2015

deal in this respect was the denationalization of the telecommunications industry.

Carlos Slim

Here the big winner was the billionaire Carlos Slim. The son of immigrants from Lebanon, he specialized in buying up companies with huge debts, turning them around, and then selling them off. However, it was during his friend Carlos Salinas de Gortari's presidency that his fortune skyrocketed, thanks mainly to his acquisition of Telmex, the then state-owned mobile telephone company, in 1991. This move is said to have doubled his fortune overnight, and propelled him into the 'top 20' of the annual list of billionaires published by *Forbes* magazine in the United States.

In Mexico City, Carlos Slim somewhat incongruously teamed up with the then left-wing mayor Andres Manuel López Obrador to help restore many buildings in the city's historic centre. He has also invested more than $1 billion on developing the district of Nuevo Polanco (more commonly known as 'Ciudad Slim') with his Museo Soumaya, luxury fashion outlets, and high-end apartments.

The effects of NAFTA

After taking office in 2000, President Fox and his PAN administration seem to have regarded the work of their pro-business government to have already been done by those who for many decades had purportedly been their political rivals. The PAN president's main aim was to maintain economic stability, keep inflation in check, and exercise tight control on government spending. This approach was relatively successful, but it became increasingly obvious that the NAFTA agreement, while it led to a huge increase in Mexican exports, boosted the numbers in unskilled labour rather than generating skilled jobs or higher wages in the Mexican economy as a whole.

Since the introduction of the NAFTA agreement, more than 80 per cent of Mexican exports have gone to the United States. As a result, when the global financial crisis struck Mexico's northern neighbour in 2008, it hit the Mexican economy even harder. In 2009, GDP fell by an estimated 6.1 per cent, and poverty

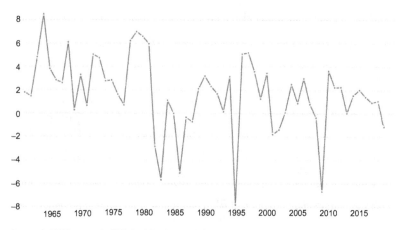

Annual GDP growth (%) in Mexico, 1961–2019
Source: World Bank, 2020

levels, which had fallen thanks to social programmes set up by Presidents Zedillo (1994–2000) and Fox, climbed to over half the population once again.

During the second PAN administration, President Calderón failed in his attempts to create the hundreds of thousands of new jobs necessary to provide economic growth. Concentrating above all on his war against the drug cartels, he baulked at carrying out needed reforms in the oil sector, tax structures, and regional imbalances, so that the annual economic growth rate during his presidency was little more than 1 per cent.

PEMEX

Since the mid-1970s, the state oil and gas concern PEMEX had provided the government with up to a quarter of its revenues in taxes and export earnings. It had also given employment to some 150,000 Mexicans, most of them organized in the all-powerful STPRM (Sindicato de Trabajadores Petroleros de la República Mexicana, the Union of Mexican Petroleum Industry Workers) union. Seen as a key component of Mexico's revolutionary nationalism since its creation in 1938, over the years PEMEX became a byword for mismanagement, inefficiency, and corruption. But successive governments, PRI or PAN, had found it was too potent a symbol, and too powerful a company, to be able to reform in any meaningful way.

PEMEX's oil production reached a peak of 3.4 million barrels per day in 2004, but a decade later this had declined to 2.5 million bpd, and the company's capacity to open up new fields or to restructure itself plummeted. As a consequence, when the PRI's new young president, Enrique Peña Nieto came to power in 2012, he turned his back on his party's traditional support for the company that signified 'Mexico's oil for the Mexicans'. He introduced a constitutional reform intended to end its seven decade monopoly once and for all. Passed in December 2013, this reform provided competition and foreign investment in every area of the oil and gas industry, from exploration to the opening up of sales of petrol at the pump, all of them previously in the hands of PEMEX. This led foreign firms to bid to explore for new deposits, and discoveries that attracted major international oil firms.

'Rescuing sovereignty'

However, when his successor AMLO took office in 2018, he signalled a reversal of these efforts to introduce competition into the Mexican oil and gas industry. He appears to view the importance of PEMEX as a symbol of Mexico's sovereignty as more vital to the country than any increase in its efficiency, or the transparency of its operations. He has rebranded its logo with the slogan 'Rescuing Sovereignty', and one of his first moves after coming into office was to suspend any new oil field auctions for at least three years. Although he vowed to increase PEMEX's production, in 2019 it fell to no more than 1.7 million bpd. This meant it only contributed some 11 per cent to government revenues, less than half that of earlier years.

AMLO's economic strategy unravelled early in 2020, with the collapse of the international oil price, and the disastrous effects on consumption of the Covid-19 virus. In March 2020, PEMEX reported a quarterly loss of $23 billion, and total debts of $105 billion, making it the most indebted oil company in the world. Instead of being, as AMLO boasted, the motor of Mexico's economy and the guarantor of its 'energy independence', it now appears that even before the effects of Covid-19 are factored in, it will require some 3 per cent of GDP spent on PEMEX annually over the next few years simply to keep the company afloat.

Maquilas

Apart from oil and gas, the chief contributor to Mexico's export earnings has come from the enormous *maquila* or assembly plant industries mostly located close to the US border in cities such as Tijuana and Ciudad Juárez. Begun in the 1960s to offer jobs to Mexican workers returning from the United States after the closure of the *bracero* programme, the *maquilas* are now estimated to employ more than a million people. These plants import raw materials and semi-finished goods duty free. The products are assembled and then exported again, with little tax paid on the finished items. The 3,000 or so *maquilas* churn out everything from apparel to cars and electronic components, with Japanese, South Korean, and Chinese firms now joining US companies to take advantage of the low taxes paid and cheap Mexican labour (average wages are under $2.50 an hour).

In recent years more than 65 per cent of Mexico's exports have come from these assembly plants. Employment in the *maquilas*, though generally offering only low wages, is regarded in Mexico as relatively stable. This has exacerbated the population drift from the poorer southern states. Often these migrant workers are chaotically housed, with inadequate infrastructure, overcrowding, and the almost constant threat of violence.

Of course, many poor Mexicans do not stop on the Mexican side of the border, but try by any means possible to cross into the United States. In spite of successive attempts by Washington to limit this flow, by now there are reckoned to be 37 million first or second generation Mexicans living in the United States, or about 11 per cent of the total population. Many of these are young men who do seasonal work in the north, then return to their villages in Mexico for the winter months. Millions though have stayed, and become US citizens, but still send back money to their relatives: in 2019 these remittances totalled more than $36 billion.

Tourism

Another sector vital to the Mexican economy is tourism, which accounts for some 17 per cent of its GDP and 20 per cent of its foreign earnings. The past 40 years have seen the promotion of mega-resorts on both the Pacific and Atlantic coasts, often to the detriment of the environment and local communities. Almost 25 million foreign tourists now visit Mexico each year, but once again, the business is extremely susceptible to external shocks, especially those affecting the United States. In 2008–2009 due to the worldwide financial crisis and an outbreak of swine fever in Mexico, the huge resort of Cancún on the Yucatán peninsula almost closed down completely. Mexican tourism officials estimated that 5 million fewer tourists entered Mexico in that year. More recently, the drugs related violence widely reported abroad has led to once glamorous resorts such as Acapulco seeing a huge reduction in foreign visitors.

The effects of the 2020 Covid-19 virus are likely to be even more devastating. International travel is set to shrink by perhaps 50 per cent for the foreseeable future, and AMLO's uncertain handling of the crisis will inevitably put off many tourists, particularly those from north of the border.

AMLO in power

When AMLO won the July 2018 election, the arrival of a left-wing 'firebrand' to the presidency immediately provoked capital flight and gave the Mexican stock market the jitters. But when he took office in December 2018, he calmed fears that he would seek to increase public spending to ensure popularity. To demonstrate a new austerity in public life, he cut his own salary by more than half, and insisted that top civil servants and judges (very reluctantly) did the same. He attempted to sell the 80 seat presidential plane that Peña Nieto had bought at the start of his presidency, instead taking commercial flights for his many trips around the country. Unfortunately, there were no takers for the purchase, and so the Boeing Dreamliner is set to be the star prize in a national raffle.

As part of this austerity drive, thousands of government workers were dismissed, while many more have faced wage cuts. The incoming president cancelled the construction of a new airport for Mexico City at Texcoco (already one third completed), due to cost more than $13 billion. He argued that this was a typical product of the 'corrupt' regimes that went before him, with fat government contracts being awarded to a small number of companies (including those of his old friend Carlos Slim), little attention being paid to its environmental impact, and foreign investment that would lead to further debt problems for Mexico.

To demonstrate support for this cancellation of the new airport, he held a *consulta popular*, in which the electorate was asked to vote and give their opinion – another of the means by which AMLO hopes to deepen Mexico's democracy. Although only a million voters turned out, the vast majority were in favour of the cancellation of what the president described as a 'pharaonic' project.

Instead, AMLO proposed adapting the Santa Lucia military airbase in nearby Zumpango, which he claimed would be cheaper and more useful. His critics called this 'AMLO's flying white elephant', arguing it would cost more to compensate investors in the original project than to continue with its construction. By May 2020, with air traffic down by almost 85 per cent in Mexico as a result of the Covid-19 virus, and with recovery to today's levels seen as years away, the Santa Lucia airport appears superfluous to requirements.

During his campaign, AMLO vowed he would devote his efforts to improving the lives of Mexico's poor millions. He has brought in a substantial increase in the minimum wage, improved labour rights for domestic workers, and introduced direct cash transfers to the elderly, people with disabilities, and students. He also launched an ambitious apprenticeship scheme called *jovenes construyendo el futuro* (young people building the future) to offer employment for many thousands of young Mexicans without academic qualifications.

At the same time, however, he has proposed expensive megaprojects of his own. These include the Tren Maya in the southernmost states, intended to improve communications there and attract tourists. He also announced the construction of a huge new oil refinery at Dos Bocas in his home state of Tabasco, aimed at boosting PEMEX's refinery capacity. The weakness of the projects, his critics insist, is that the president appears to think that PEMEX can generate revenues as it did in the 'glory years' of the 40s and 50s to finance them, whereas everything points to the state oil and gas concern becoming increasingly out-of-date and unprofitable.

Internationally, AMLO pushed through the renegotiation of NAFTA with Canada and the United States begun in August 2017 after US President Trump threatened to withdraw from what he called 'the worst trade deal in history'. The new agreement, catchily called USMCA, in fact saw the continuation of most of the provisions of the earlier accord, although President Trump could claim that some of the production of cars and other goods will now revert to the United States. In Mexico, there is to be a reinforcement of labour and environmental protection, while more goods and services will be tariff-free across the three countries, in an effort to boost trade.

In the third decade of the 21st century, Mexico is one of the world's biggest 15 economies, and the largest one in emerging nations after the BRIC countries. However, in 2019 economic growth was minimal, and GDP actually contracted in the last quarter. Before the outbreak of the Covid-19 virus, forecasters had predicted growth of only a little over 1 per cent for the next two years, well below the annual 4 per cent growth that AMLO had promised on his campaign trail.

More than 50 million people (42 per cent of the population) are classified as living in poverty, and perhaps a third of the population in extreme poverty. More worryingly, among Mexico's indigenous communities, particularly in the south of the country, that figure rises to almost three-quarters of the population. There is also a huge wealth disparity, with the top 10 per cent of Mexicans possessing 42 per cent of national wealth, as compared to 1.3 per cent of national wealth owned by the bottom 10 per cent (according to World Bank estimates).

Worse still, in May 2020, the government agency for social development gave a sombre forecast that the effects of the Covid-19 virus could lead to an increase in the number of those living in poverty by almost 11 million, the vast majority of them in Mexico's already overcrowded cities. Already in April 2020 an estimated half a million Mexicans had lost their jobs in the formal sector of the economy, and many thousands more in the informal one. External trade dropped by 41 per cent in the same month, and GDP was estimated to have shrunk by 2.2 per cent. The president who came to power promising a bright economic future for his country will have his work cut out over the remaining four years in office to rescue it from economic meltdown.

Tortillas: still a Mexican staple (Sebastián Machado)

7 Culture

Mexican cultural life today draws on a heritage going back more than 3,000 years. It's not uncommon for this past to break through to the surface, as with the Aztec Templo Major (Great Temple) right in the heart of Mexico City. The remains of the temple were only revealed in February 1978, when workmen laying electricity cables unearthed the corner of what turned out to be the extensive walls of the main place of Aztec worship. This was the religious centre that so impressed the Spanish conquistadors during their invasion of Tenochtitlan, the Aztec capital. The Templo Mayor has been excavated and is now on view next to the Spanish colonial cathedral, itself built directly on top of other Aztec temples.

More discoveries have followed: the latest was the 2018 unearthing of the *tzompantli* or 'wall of skulls', made up of hundreds of skulls of men, women, and children. The extent to which the Aztecs indulged in human sacrifice has long been the subject of debate: this new discovery seems to prove that they did put to death many of those rival groups they defeated in battle. Other new archaeological finds continue all over Mexico: a new important Mayan site was uncovered in 2019 in north-eastern Yucatán, a hundred miles from Cancún, and is still being worked on.

Heritage of the past

Rightly proud of this heritage, the Mexican state has made great efforts to preserve and promote these civilizations from the distant past: the Toltecs, Mayans, Aztecs, and many other precious sites, mainly thanks to the government agency INAH (Instituto Nacional de Antropologia e Historia). Mexico City's Museo de Antropología (Anthropological Museum) displays sculptures, other objects, and artefacts from the ancient cultures that thrived in what is now modern-day Mexico. They are housed and explained in a superb 1960s building by the architect Pedro Ramírez Vázquez, with the spectacular Tree of Life at its centre. Museums in many other regional cities exhibit finds from local areas.

The three centuries of Spanish colonial rule have also left many monuments: palaces built from volcanic rock in the capital; churches with extravagant baroque ornamentation; lonely austere chapels in desert landscapes; paintings and handicrafts: silver in Taxco, ceramics from Puebla, and many different regional products.

People of maize

Maize gods feature in many sculptures in Mexico City's Museum of Anthropology. Archaeologists have found evidence it was cultivated in Mexico more than 5,000 years ago. Not only was maize a staple food for the earliest Mexicans, but it was an essential part of the Mayan creation myth as written down in the Popol Vuh. Then as now, food bound people together and gave them a shared identity. In ancient times, the ears of maize were boiled in lime, then ground into a paste and made into a *masa* or dough – the primitive tortilla – with chillies added to spice up the carbohydrate. So the tortillas served everywhere in Mexico today provide a link back over several thousand years, and food in Mexico is one of the most important elements of the nation's cultural identity.

As well as tortillas, Mexico has given any number of vegetables and fruits to the world: cacao to make chocolate, vanilla, tomatoes, avocadoes, papayas, turkeys, and, for the brave, *chapulines* or deep-fried grasshoppers sold as a delicacy in Oaxaca and elsewhere. Thanks to the country's geographical extension and long coastlines, the Mexican diet includes everything from tropical fruit to many kinds of fish and meat.

Mexican meals are an art form in themselves, often extending over several hours and ending in general carousing. Breakfast for example can include tortillas, frijoles or refried beans, chillies, and eggs cooked in a huge variety of ways, from *rancheros* (fried eggs, beans, cheese, avocado, hot chilli sauce) to *estrellados* (scrambled) to *divorciados* (two fried eggs, one with fresh green sauce, the other with a red one). Lunches and dinners can be of chicken with chocolate sauce (*mole*) or *pipián de pollo* (with pumpkin seeds), pork or chicken *tamales* (steamed in a maize or banana leaf), stewed beef or *chivito* (goat), and for the most adventurous, iguanas, still eaten in the south of the country.

There is also every kind of seafood, from shrimp to shark. To accompany any meal there are more than a hundred varieties of chilli peppers, ranging from the relatively mild *jalapeño* to the incandescent *habanero*.

In short, Mexicans take their food very seriously, from street markets (where the unwary tourist will soon learn the meaning of 'Moctezuma's revenge') to Michelin-starred restaurants in Mexico City and other big cities.

Cantina culture

A more questionable tradition is the wide array of drinks that Mexicans consume. These range from rotgut *pulque* and *mezcal* to hundreds of brands of more refined tequila. *Mezcal,* made from the fermented juice of the maguey cactus, is the national tipple, usually drunk with the inclusion of a *gusano* or worm (in fact the pupa of a common moth). It is usually made by small-scale producers, traditionally in Oaxaca, whereas the more internationally known *tequila* is produced on a more industrial scale. These strong drinks are served everywhere, from the meanest *cantina* in the countryside to the most chic cocktail bars in the big cities. Mexican beer also has a well-deserved reputation,

Breakfast at Sanborns (Valeria Arendar)

while *atole,* a cloying cinnamon drink with a maize base, is often served as a restorative after too much alcohol.

Mexican wine, which for many years was undrinkable, is also seeing something of a renaissance thanks to investment from abroad and fresh vineyards. Nearly all the production is in Baja California. It was here that Jesuits originally planted vines in the 17th century, until the jealous Spanish crown prohibited the sale of Mexican wine in order to protect Spanish producers. Nowadays the Valle de Guadalupe in Baja California is the centre of a booming industry, with tourists encouraged to travel the length of the valley, stopping off at the vineyards.

Cultural revolution

In the 20th century, the strong nationalist spirit following the 1910 revolution was the dominant force in everything from architecture (Mexico City's Monument to the Revolution and the Fine Arts Palace are notable examples) to literature, music and painting. In music, Silvestre Revueltas and Carlos Chávez created new music out of popular folk tunes. In painting, the new spirit of national pride is most obvious in the public mural art promoted by the 1920s education minister José Vasconcelos and created by Diego Rivera, Clemente Orozco, David Siqueiros, and others. They depicted the 'paradise' of pre-Columbian life and its destruction first by the Spaniards and later by the rapacious capitalist system on the walls and ceilings of public buildings such as Mexico City's Ministry of Education or the Palacio de Gobierno in Guadalajara. This idea of educating through pictures has parallels with the Christian tradition of telling the Bible stories for often illiterate church goers.

Not everyone appreciated these grandiose creations: the English novelist D.H. Lawrence, who visited Mexico after the revolution in the 1920s, wrote in his novel *The Plumed Serpent:* 'They were ugly and vulgar. Strident caricatures of the Capitalist and the Church and of Mammon, painted life-size and as violent as possible, round the patio of the grey old building where the young people are educated. To anyone with a spark of human balance they are a misdemeanour.'

In recent years many Mexicans have come to share a similar view, and fashion in art has swung much more to the side of Rivera's partner Frida Kahlo, with her private, anguished paintings

Frida Kahlo's wheelchair in the Casa Azul (Linda Etchart)

that reject any grandiloquence. Frida Kahlo has become an international icon of feminist suffering and artistic triumph over pain (and the value of her paintings has skyrocketed thanks to the singer Madonna collecting them).

Nevertheless, public art has remained a strong tradition in Mexico: Rufino Tamayo also painted huge murals, for example in the UNESCO building in Paris, but with a less didactic and more personal style. Another painter who placed great importance on the artist's public role was the Oaxacan master Francisco Toledo, who died in 2019. He frequently combined his art with the defence of indigenous groups and other social movements: shortly before his death he designed 43 kites as a reminder of the same number of students who disappeared in the 2014 Ayotzinapa massacre.

A new generation of painters has embraced international styles and experimentation, while public art nowadays tends to be found in graffiti on the walls of streets in cities and villages throughout Mexico. Graphic art in woodcuts and lithographs is also a strong tradition in Mexico that stretches back to artists like José Guadalupe Posada, who during the revolution worked incessantly in his workshop in the centre of Mexico City depicting life and death around him. He was the creator of the world famous *calaveras* or dancing skeletons that mock the pretensions of the living.

Books and reading

State promotion of education and reading in the 1920s and 1930s, with the creation of the Fondo de Cultura Económica in 1934 to print and supply good cheap books, was part of a determined effort to spread literacy throughout the country. There's a common saying in Mexico that if you pick up any stone you'll find a poet underneath, and in the 20th and 21st centuries there has been a wealth of important poetic voices in Mexico.

The most prominent voices in the years after the revolution were Alfonso Reyes and the much younger Octavio Paz. His insistence on the primacy of poetry and poetic imagination made his many collections essential reading both inside Mexico and abroad, although paradoxically perhaps his most widely read book *El laberinto de la soledad* (*The Labyrinth of Solitude*, first published in 1950) is a prose reflection on Mexican identity that had enormous influence. More recently a younger generation of poets have explored more personal themes as the idea of the poet as public figure with an important role to play in defining the nation has dwindled.

The revolution also inspired a whole series of novels, beginning with the groundbreaking *Los de abajo (The Underdogs)* written by Mariano Azuela as early as 1916. Many of these fictional works used the revolutionary struggle as the backdrop to the foundation of a new nation and a new order. Later novelists such as Carlos Fuentes (the best-known Mexican contributor to the so-called 'boom' of Latin American writing in the 1960s and 70s), continued to examine the legacy of the revolution in books such as *La muerte de Artemio Cruz (The Death of Artemio Cruz*, first published in 1962). While Fuentes produced more than 20 novels, as well as short stories and essays, Juan Rulfo (1917–1986) made his name in Mexico and abroad with just two books: *Pedro Páramo* (1955), an elegy for the dying rural world, and *El llano en llamas (The Burning Plain*, 1958). These slender volumes have stood the test of time much better than more grandiose efforts. Other writers such as José Revueltas, José Agustín or Elena Poniatowska (*La noche de Tlatelolco – The Night of Tlatelolco*, 1971) saw the 1968 student massacre in Mexico City as proof of the rottenness of the PRI system, and were openly critical of what they saw as the failures of Mexican society. Another keen observer and critic of the society around him was Carlos Monsivais, who dissected everyday life in Mexico and its institutions with a keen, mocking eye. This critical observation has been continued by Juan Villoro, while the drug wars have led to the appearance (as in popular music) of a whole genre of narco-thrillers written by authors such as Elmer Mendoza, whose novels are set in Culiacán, a centre for drugs violence.

Mexican women writers have also been prominent and successful, from Rosario Castellanos and her exploration of the indigenous world, to Poniatowska, Margo Glantz, and Carmen Boullosa. In the 21st century, these outstanding female figures have been joined by a newer generation that is winning international acclaim: Valeria Luiselli, Guadalupe Nettel, and Fernanda Melchor among many others.

Together with Argentina, Mexico has traditionally been one of the most important centres for the publishing industry in Latin America. Mexico City and the other large cities boast many eclectic bookshops, and each year Guadalajara hosts Latin America's largest book fair with hundreds of thousands of visitors, and yet outside the urban centres support for reading is often still weak.

Handicrafts

Throughout the 20th century, successive governments have also supported the production of handicrafts from all the different states. Many of them have *tiendas* in Mexico City and other big cities, where regional artefacts are displayed and are on sale. Ceramics, gold and silverwork, leather and other goods are also to be found in huge quantities in the craft markets in every city and town. A recent addition are the *alebrijes,* or *papier mâché* monsters made up of three different kinds of imaginary animal. Originally the creation of one man, Pedro Linares López, who said he dreamt of them in a vision during a serious illness, they are now produced by many different craft workers, and are the main attraction of a parade of *alebrijes monumentales* organized by the Museo de Arte Popular in Mexico City every October.

Kitchen earthenware (Linda Etchart)

Photography and film

In addition to painting and handicrafts, photography has long been an important art form in Mexico. Introduced in the mid-19th century by early French photography pioneers, studio portraits soon became all the rage (plus the very Mexican tradition of photographs of dead babies or *angelitos*). Alongside this was a growing interest in photographing Mexico's architectural and natural heritage, as captured by photographers like Hugo Brehme and Frida's father, Guillermo Kahlo. However, it was during the years of revolution that photography came into its own, with the Casasola family making thousands of images that brought the conflict to life in the newspapers of the time. They took vivid snapshots of everything during that tumultuous decade, from the women *soldaderas* who followed their men folk into battle to portraits of the revolutionary heroes (the Casasola archive is now housed in a former convent in Pachuca).

The interest in photography continued in the 1930s, with the Italian-Mexican Tina Modotti and the world-renowned Manuel Alvarez Bravo producing iconic images. As the writer Carlos Monsivais has complained, Mexican photographers have sometimes fallen into the trap of portraying '*indios bonitos*' or tear-jerking images of 'filthy-faced children' in poverty, but the best of more recent photographers, such as Graciela Iturbide with her *Women of Juchitán,* Flor Garduño or Gerardo Suter and others have continued to roam Mexico in search of images that are a true reflection of everyday life. There is also a strong tradition of street photography for newspapers or magazines, epitomized by the work of Nacho López and many others.

Mexican cinema has also been very successful internationally recently, with *Roma* (named after the now fashionable middle-class neighbourhood in Mexico City – Colonia Roma) winning the first Oscar for a Mexican film in 2019 and others such as *Amores Perros* directed by Alejandro González Iñárritu (who also won Academy awards for the 2015 film *Birdman*) and Guillermo del Toro finding praise and audiences internationally. But it was the 1940s and 1950s that saw the heyday of Mexican cinema, before the distribution of Hollywood films swamped the market. Film stars like María Félix or Dolores del Río, or the male heart throbs Pedro Infante and Jorge Negrete, plus comedians such as Tintán or Cantinflas were idols for a whole generation of Mexicans.

Many of the songs from these 1940s and 1950s films were immensely popular on Mexican radio. Migrants from the countryside to towns and cities relied on broadcasts of regional music to remind them nostalgically of what they had left behind: the *corridos* that began in the years of revolution, *ranchera* music, *boleros* and romantic ballads, sung in the 1930s by the archetypal crooner Agustín Lara, and followed by many others such as Vicente Fernández, or the incomparable Chavela Vargas. Best-known internationally and also very popular in Mexico itself are the *mariachi* bands, small groups of musicians with the huge *guitarrón* and blaring trumpets who offer to play at fiestas, birthday parties, and other celebrations. Nowadays a new variant on the *corrido* music sung by groups such as Los Tigres del Norte (who successfully took *norteño* music to the United States and made their homes there) has emerged: the *narcocorridos*, songs that tell stories of drug traffickers and their adventures, and how ordinary people get caught up in tragic situations.

Pop and rock music

While much of this music stirs nostalgic memories, the history of music aimed at the young in Mexico has been a troubled one. The first Mexican rock song broadcast on the radio is said to have been by Los Rebeldes del Rock in 1959. By the end of the 1960s, following the Tlatelolco massacre, a strong musical counterculture known as '*la onda*' grew up, critical of the government and older generations. In 1971 the 'Mexican Woodstock', (the Avándaro festival) was held near Toluca, with a two-day audience of more than 300,000 young people. President Luis Echeverria's government was so concerned about possible social unrest that after this event it severely restricted the production and airtime of rock music, both Mexican and foreign. Hard metal groups and Mexican punk bands played in small venues called '*hoyos fonqui*'. Since then, Mexican pop and rock music or *rock nacional* by bands such as Café Tacuba has won increasing audiences, and Mexican groups have had great success throughout Latin America as well as with their compatriots in the United States.

Popular fiestas

Many Mexican cities and towns still have a central square or *plaza* with a formal garden and in the middle a wrought-iron or wooden bandstand. Particularly in the south, on hot nights locals stroll round the square (in the past, the men went one way, and women the other, eyeing each other). This is where the many boisterous fiestas take place, with fireworks and the town band playing dance music to celebrate the local saint's day, independence, or one of the other many excuses for a party. Then the bandstands and gardens are decorated with boldly coloured flags and pennants, and many of the older people dance the *danzón,* a slow waltz-like dance brought to the eastern port of Veracruz from Cuba but now thoroughly Mexicanized.

The most famous of these fiestas is the celebration of the Día de los Muertos, the Day of the Dead. This event takes place over two days at the start of November, coinciding with the Catholic Day of Saints and Day of Souls. This is when families throughout Mexico decorate altars at home and eat sweet bread rolls or *pan del muerto* in honour of their dead relatives. The following day they visit their tombs in cemeteries throughout Mexico. They bring offerings of the dead person's favourite food, drink, cigarettes,

Saturday morning *danzón* (Valeria Arendar)

and flowers, especially bright orange marigolds and sugar skulls to honour the deceased. A lot of drinking goes on, and there is loud, celebratory music: far from being a solemn, mournful occasion, Mexicans manage to convert the idea of death into a happy occasion when the living feel in direct contact with their beloved dead. At Easter, another tradition is the '*quema de Judas*' (the burning of Judas). These *papier mâché* figures are often very elaborate creations, often representing politicians or other people in the news.

Lucha libre

On the borderline between entertainment and sport is wrestling or *lucha libre*, long a favourite with poorer sectors of Mexican society. Each bout is a fight between good and evil, and since good usually triumphs, it provides some solace for people whose ordinary lives may not have such a reassuring outcome. Often the wrestlers wear masks – a tradition that began in the 1930s when wrestling was imported from the United States and one of the wrestlers wished to stay anonymous. The most famous *lucha libre* champion was, appropriately enough, El Santo, who never had his mask snatched off him in almost 40 years of combats. The mask and costume escaped outside the ring in the 1980s, when following the disastrous 1985 Mexico City earthquake a popular champion known as *Superbarrio* went round in mask and full spandex gear supporting solidarity initiatives. More recently, masked women wrestlers have also become a huge hit with the many fans who crowd into traditional venues such as the Arena México in Mexico City, or appear on the weekly TV shows devoted to the sport.

Fútbol

Although *lucha libre* has its devotees, as with everywhere in Latin America it is football that dominates sporting passions in Mexico. The game is said to have been introduced to Mexico by Cornish miners who came to the town of Pachuca north of the capital in the 19th century to work in the silver mines. They introduced two novelties to Mexico – Cornish pasties (people from Pachuca still know them as *los pastes*, and the city boasts dozens of Cornish pasty shops), and football. The local team is not now at the highest level, but all the big cities and towns have their fans for the national leagues, the yearly cup competition, and of course for the national side. The *El Tri* (from the three colours of the Mexican flag) always manage to reach the soccer World Cup finals (though Mexico has never won the cup). A game between the biggest rivals, Cruz Azul, Los Tigres, and the Pumas de la UNAM will fill the Estadio Azteca in Mexico City with 80,000 or more supporters.

Someone who is not apparently such a fan of football is President Andres Manuel López Obrador. His passion is for another sport: baseball. He has been a follower since his childhood in Tabasco, where there was a local league, even though baseball never really caught on in Mexico as it did in Cuba and Venezuela. Nowadays most baseball teams are based in the cities up near the US border, but AMLO hopes the game will now catch on throughout the nation. During his first year in office, he set up an Office for the Promotion and Development of Baseball, supported by some $19 million funding; his efforts seem to have borne fruit, as attendances at games are reported to have increased by as much as a third.

Mexican football's Cup Final (Valeria Arendar)

Cloud forest vegetation in El Cielo Biosphere (Mexican Tourist Board)

8 Environment

Mexico is the third-largest country in Latin America. Its territory extends over almost two million square kilometres, ranging from deserts in the north, the volcanic central region, down to hot rainforests and swamps in the south, inside the Tropic of Cancer. It is also the third most biologically diverse country on earth. US journalist Joel Simon writes in his book *Endangered Mexico*: 'it has more than 30,000 species of plants, of which 50 to 60 per cent are found nowhere else on earth...There are 255 species of amphibians, 449 mammals, 694 species of reptiles, more than 1,000 kinds of birds, 2,000 kinds of fish, and 100,000 insects, many of which have not been catalogued.'

And yet, as Joel Simon points out, this diversity is under serious threat, almost entirely from the activities of man. From air pollution in the big cities, to water shortages, soil erosion and over-farming in rural areas, the destruction of precious coastlines by the development of huge tourist resorts, the illegal logging of its rainforests, the consequences of large-scale mining and the oil industry, Mexico's environmental problems are massive.

Mining

When Marta Velarde woke up on 6 August 2014, she could hardly believe her eyes. 'The water was running orange, red, a coppery colour through the entire Rio Sonora', she told reporters. The polluted water came from a broken pipe carrying 11 million gallons of copper sulphate solution from a mine owned by Buenavista del Cobre, a subsidiary of the giant Mexican mining firm Grupo Mexico.

Two days later, Buenavista del Cobre admitted that the toxic leak contained heavy metals such as iron, aluminium and zinc, in what the then head of Mexico's Secretary for the Environment and Natural Resources José Guerra Abad called 'the worst environmental disaster caused by the mining industry in modern times'. It took the local authorities several more days to close the wells carrying the contaminated water into thousands of people's homes as drinking water.

The copper mine, near Cananea and six other small towns downstream of the mine's tailing ponds in Sonora state (some 20 miles from the Mexico–US border), has some of the largest copper reserves in Mexico. It also contains huge deposits of zinc and silver. As with other open-cast mines, at Cananea ore is blasted out of the mountainside, crushed, and the precious metals extracted using sulphuric and other acids. After this process, the toxic liquids are held in tailing dams.

As many as 22,000 locals were left without drinking water for weeks. More than 80 local schools were shut down. Most of those affected by the toxic spill were small farmers. Not only did they and their farm animals begin to suffer serious health problems, but they found it almost impossible to sell their produce as customers feared becoming contaminated as well. Grupo Mexico, the world's fourth largest mining company, owned by the billionaire Larrea family, at first claimed the accident was due to heavier than normal rainfall. Eventually, under pressure from

Cananea mine (Grupo Mexico)

environmental groups, they admitted that 'one relevant factor of the accident was a construction defect in the seal of the pipe' that led to the massive leak.

According to the Spanish news agency EFE, the Mexican government fined Grupo Mexico some $2 million, and ordered the company to pay more than $100 million into a trust fund for local people affected. This money was to be used to build a medical centre to care for the almost 400 people whose health was compromised – but the project was never completed, and was later abandoned. Only two of the 36 water treatment plants designed to eliminate heavy metals from the water were built as promised. According to some locals, only $20 million of the promised funds has materialized. Alberto Rojas Rueda, then head of environmental policy for Greenpeace Mexico, estimated it would take as many as 20 years to clean up the river: 'This involves not only repairing the damage, but there are also a number of substances left on the river bed and sides, which will require vast expenditure to remove', he said. He argued that if the Mexican government wants to prevent such toxic disasters in the future, 'it should strengthen environmental laws and provide the government environmental regulator with more and better inspectors to undertake random inspections, particularly at the dams associated with mines'.

'As soon as you can hold members of a company the size of Grupo Mexico responsible for contamination like this, you can be sure they will stop doing those things', Rojas Rueda told the press. 'Today, because economic sanctions are for very small amounts, the companies do not care if they cause contamination or not.'

Pasto de Conchos

A few years prior to the Cananea disaster, a subsidiary of the same company Grupo Mexico was involved in an accident at the Pasto de Conchos coal mine in the northern Coahuila state. In February 2006, 65 miners were trapped underground after a methane explosion. Rescue efforts were called off after only five days, which miners' relatives argued was far too soon. All 65 men died, and only two of their bodies were recovered. In its report on the incident, the International Labour Organization stated that the subsidiary had 'clearly failed in its obligations as owner and operator of the mine, leading to this tragic loss of life'. Families of the miners later claimed there had been no proper investigation into the tragedy, nobody held responsible, and no reparations paid. Several family members told reporters their husbands had spoken of a gas leak days before the explosion. The mine was closed indefinitely – Grupo Mexico claiming it had 'voluntarily' returned it to the government. In February 2020, President AMLO announced the authorities would begin a fresh attempt to recover the 63 dead bodies.

For centuries, mining has been both a source of immense wealth for Mexico and a curse for its environment and for loss of life. The history of mining in Mexico is strewn with similar stories: danger and dreadful working conditions for those working in the mines, and huge profits for the owners. During the three centuries of Spanish rule, it has been estimated that billions of dollars' worth of gold, silver, and other precious metals were shipped from Mexico back to Spain, while only a handful of people in Mexico enjoyed the wealth generated. At the same time, the mining industry has provided employment for many thousands of Mexicans living in areas of the country, especially the northern states, where until now there have been few other job opportunities.

The mining industry was one of the main beneficiaries of the neo-liberal policies of the final PRI governments at the end of the 20th century, and of the NAFTA agreement that came into force in 1994. Deregulation meant that as much as 28 per cent of Mexican territory was made available for new mining ventures. As in other sectors of the economy, it was Canadian and US firms that in the main were able to benefit from this opening, due to their lengthy experience and scale of investment. Environmental groups in Mexico have consistently complained that these companies have taken advantage of the lack of regulation by the Mexican authorities to bypass safety and environmental precautions.

The fragile coastline

The Mexican oil industry offers a prime example of the costs to the environment of a hugely important industry. The 1979 oil blowout of the Ixtoc 1 well in the Gulf of Mexico sent the equivalent of 3.4 million barrels of crude oil into a pristine marine ecosystem. The leaking oil continued to pollute the sea and the nearby coastline for several months, and its effects on underwater life, fishing, and the adjacent coast, are still being felt today. Until BP's Deepwater Horizon explosion in 2010, this was the largest recorded oil spill in history.

Mexico has more than 9,000 kilometres of coastline on the Caribbean Gulf of Mexico and on the Pacific. An equally serious challenge to the coastal environment has been the way successive governments have promoted large-scale tourism and the development of huge resort complexes. These have often been financed by ex-presidents and other prominent politicians. On the Yucatán peninsula the city of Cancún and the Riviera Maya have been massively developed in recent years with little regard for the environmental consequences. Similarly on the Pacific coast a resort city like Puerto Vallarta has grown from a small town of 20,000 people a generation ago, to close to half a million nowadays. It has more than 40 luxury hotels, welcomes huge cruise ships, and has its own airport. A 1993 law allowed foreigners to buy land in the region, and this led to the loss of most of the commonly owned *ejidos,* and the influx of thousands of pensioners from the United States and Canada, while levels of poverty among the local population increased significantly.

Karmina Palace resort at Manzanillo (Jack Borno)

All these developments put pressure on a unique geological land-scape and coastline, destroying habitats, flora and fauna, and delicate ecosystems.

Cabo Pulmo

Since in Mexico big business interests are far more powerful than environmental NGOs and groups, success stories in preventing such developments are rare. One notable exception has been Cabo Pulmo on the southern tip of Baja California, the home to one of the very few living coral reefs in North America. Some 400 species of fish are found there, from different kinds of shark, manta rays, groupers, and many other species.

Cabo Pulmo was a traditional fishing village, which faced its first crisis in the 1990s when overfishing meant the abundant stocks of fish were fast disappearing. The local community accepted the challenge of turning more than 7,000 hectares of the waters off the coast into a protected nature reserve, even though this meant the fishermen were out of work for several years.

Cabo Pulmo (Mexican Tourist Board)

But protecting the marine species paid off spectacularly, so that by the turn of the 21st century stocks had not only recovered within the reserve, but also in the surrounding area. As a result, Cabo Pulmo became a huge attraction for eco-tourists, most of them wanting to go snorkelling on the reef or swim with the sharks.

Then, as in so many other stretches of the Mexican coastline, in 2008 a large international developer decided that Cabo Pulmo would be the ideal spot to create a new tourist resort. This was to be known as Cabo Cortés, with a capacity for 30,000 guest rooms, a marina, desalination plant, three golf courses, highways to bring in more tourists, and even an airstrip. Such a massive development would inevitably have produced pollution and toxic waste that would have threatened the reef's continued existence, and swamped the local community's facilities.

For once, the Mexican government's environmental agency SEMARNAT opposed the scheme, and in June 2012 the then President Felipe Calderón cancelled the project's environmental permits. Undeterred, the developers put forward other, equally massive plans for the site, and appealed the decision. It was not until September 2015 when SEMARNAT published a 100-page report outlining all the objections to the scheme that the courts finally threw out the proposal once and for all.

Choking cities

Away from the coasts, Mexico's big cities also face huge environmental challenges. The case of the capital city is emblematic. Most striking is the problem of air pollution: situated at an altitude of over 8,000 feet and in the bowl of the Valle de Mexico surrounded by mountains, the air is already rarefied. Due to also being the seat of a high proportion of the country's industry, as well as having as many as 10 million vehicles on its roads daily, air pollution is a chronic problem in the winter months from December to March when there is little rainfall. This was at its worst in the 1980s, when solutions envisaged included placing giant fans on the top of the capital's skyscrapers, and attempts were made to restrict traffic by having days when vehicles with odd/even registration plates could only be used on alternate days. The situation has since improved slightly, but rates of asthma and breathing problems are still higher than elsewhere in Latin America.

The Aztec capital of Tenochtitlán was built on a series of islands dotted around five lakes. Following the Spanish conquest, the city's population grew rapidly, and the Spanish colonizers drained the lakes. As the sandy mud dried out, the earth became unstable, and unable to support the weight of the increasing number and size of buildings. So the capital began to sink into the mud at an alarming rate. The old centre was the worst hit, and today the cathedral as well as many of the other magnificent colonial churches and palaces have sunk several feet below pavement level. The lack of stability of the subsoil is also one of the reasons why the 1985 and 2017 earthquakes were so devastating, as poorly constructed buildings toppled in the dried-out earth.

As well as the problem of sinking into the former lake beds, the Mexican capital has also suffered for centuries from the opposite problem. During the Spanish colonial period, floods were almost routine, as the city is in a valley surrounded by mountains, meaning that rain and waste water have no immediate outlet. The Spaniards attempted to solve this problem by digging a tunnel through the mountains so that the water could escape down to the Pacific. This solution was always inadequate, and floods continued until at least the middle of the 20th century. In recent years, a deep drainage system has been developed, which has coped until now.

Water wars

Water supplies are also crucial in the semi-desert states of the north of the country. Irrigation at the northern border depends on the flow of two rivers: the Colorado River in the west, and the famous Rio Bravo (known north of the border as the Rio Grande), which forms the border between the two countries for almost 3,000 kilometres. The flow of these crucial rivers is regulated by a series of dams, and since a 1944 treaty water supplies to the neighbouring countries have been regulated by a bi-national entity, the International Boundary and Water Commission. In recent years, the flow of the Colorado River has diminished by almost 20 per cent, leaving the thousands of Mexican farmers who rely on it for water to wonder how long their lands will be fertile.

Twenty-five years ago, Texan farmers protested that Mexico was not complying with the amounts of water it was supposed to supply the United States from tributaries to the Rio Grande. Although tensions have eased since 2016 when Mexico repaid its 'water debt', both sides are anxious about the effects that global warming could have on river levels over the coming decades, with fears that desert conditions could spread, driving more small farmers off the land and into the big cities.

Monarch butterflies

Mexico is home to some 10 per cent of the world's flora and fauna, but many of its unique habitats and ecosystems are under threat. The best-known example of this concerns the Monarch butterflies. Each year, millions of these beautiful orange and black butterflies travel thousands of kilometres south from Canada in wintertime and cluster in valleys and forests in the Mexican states of Michoacán and the state of Mexico. According to wildlife experts, the Monarch numbers have declined more than 80 per cent in the past two decades. Illegal logging of the oyamel evergreen trees in the Mexican host forests has greatly reduced the area where the butterflies can settle. Scientists have also warned that global warming could mean that the Monarchs settle much farther north in Canada, and that their winter migration flight to Mexico will be in jeopardy.

Further south, in the jungle areas of Chiapas and the Yucatán peninsula, illegal logging and clearing of the forest for large scale agriculture has been the biggest threat to not only the wildlife but also the whole way of life of local, mainly indigenous, communities. In addition, as in many other countries, the number of devastating forest fires that have occurred throughout Mexico in recent years has led to a major loss of habitat.

The Tren Maya

Early on in his *sexenio*, President López Obrador caused a storm of protest among many indigenous groups in the southern states of Mexico with his announcement of the construction of the Tren Maya. This 1,500-kilometre railway from Cancún in the Yucatàn peninsula to Palenque, one of the major Mayan sites in Chiapas, is designed to open up the area for trade and tourism. However, local communities as well as environmental groups have argued that it will threaten their way of life and their livelihoods, as well as causing massive destruction to the rainforest and animal and plant life. 'These lines could be very harmful for nature, not just because of the effects of the train itself, but above all because of the growth in population and infrastructure in the region, which could devastate natural resources', said Casandra Reyes García, of the Yucatán Scientific Research Centre.

In November 2018, a large number of Mexican academics sent the president a letter warning that a project of this size could not be undertaken without a thorough review of its ecological, cultural, and archaeological impact. Their letter emphasized that 'sites of great biodiversity must be preserved according to the strictest international standards, recognizing the wisdom of the original people who have always been guarantors of these territories and trustees of our country's natural and cultural wealth.'

According to Pesident López Obrador, the train will mainly use existing lines built in the last century. 'No land will be expropriated, no small properties, no farm co-operatives. And 50,000 hectares of fruit trees will be planted', he told reporters. The Tren Maya, among other infrastructure initiatives by the president, was put to a nationwide referendum on 24–25 November 2018. The referendum has been criticized both for the haste with which it was organized, and because only 850,527 Mexican voters took part, less than 1 per cent of those eligible to vote. Local experts also claim the referendum violated international accords, in particular ILO (International Labour Organization) Agreement 169, which stipulates that governments are obliged to undertake prior consultation with indigenous groups over any measure of this kind affecting them, and that they are the ones who must decide the priorities of any such initiative.

For its part, the EZLN (Zapatista National Liberation Army) based in Chiapas, who are long-time critics of López Obrador, declared their rejection of not only the Tren Maya but other megaprojects proposed by the new government. On 1 January 2019, 25 years since its first appearance, EZLN subcomandante Moisés declared that the Zapatistas would fight these proposals, and that they would not allow López Obrador 'to come here with his destructive projects'.

In official documents, the government explains that the Tren Maya, work on which began in mid-2020 and is due to be completed by 2022, is an 'integrated project for regional development that aims to boost the economy through tourism and local initiatives, strengthen social development, promote and safeguard Mayan culture, and protect the environment'. But on 13 February 2019, in the national Chamber of Deputies, Environment Minister Josefa González Blanco admitted that the environmental impact of the Tren Maya was as yet unknown. Shortly before her declaration, the director of the National Tourist Board, Rogelio Jiménez Pons, caused controversy when he declared that development was bound to affect the natural environment: 'We won't get anywhere if we have fat jaguars and starving children', he said in defence of the project.

Environmental policies

As with many areas of life in Mexico, there is a huge gap between official environmental policy and what actually happens on the ground. Mexico's first environment minister was appointed by President Salinas in 1994, but the ministry has often lacked the power or the resources to curb abuses. In mining and other sectors, big companies simply disregard the sanctions, which are frequently too small to force them to comply. Unfortunately, this is especially true in the poorer regions that are rich in terms of the environment but lack the resources (and in many cases the will) to enforce regulations created at the federal level.

In 2012 a national climate change law was introduced, to be fully implemented in 2018. After Brazil, Mexico is the second largest emitter of CO_2 in Latin America, and so under the provisions of the law, the Mexican government pledged to reduce emissions by 50 per cent below 2000 levels by 2050. The law also states that 35 per cent of Mexico's electricity should be provided from renewable sources by 2024, and requires the biggest polluters to report regularly on compliance. A commission was set up to oversee implementation of the law's requirements, and a carbon-trading scheme was also outlined.

This initiative was followed up in 2013 when PRI President Enrique Peña Nieto brought in energy reform legislation. This increased competition, and crucially set out incentives designed to promote the development of renewable energy sources. Subsequently, official estimates state that a quarter of electricity produced in 2018 was from renewable sources such as hydro power, wind energy, or solar panels. Sometimes this drive for alternative energy sources can lead to further land disputes, as in the Tehuantepec isthmus, where small farmers have protested they are being forced off their properties by big wind farm owners.

Another of the provisions of the law included a National Climate Change Strategy intended to shape government policies up to 2050 and beyond. However, since coming to power at the end of 2018, President López Obrador has backtracked on these commitments. He has put greater emphasis on traditional fossil fuels, and hampered the growth of alternative energy sources.

In addition to these domestic measures, successive Mexican governments have played a leading role in international debates on how to deal with the problem of global warming. Mexico was quick to ratify the 2012 Kyoto Protocol and the 2016 Paris Climate Change agreement. On the other hand, Mexico relies heavily on exports of oil and gas to bolster government revenues and create employment, and, like other oil-producing nations, the current government has shown little appetite for taking a lead in reducing them.

9 Violence and drugs

One of the most tragic consequences of the Mexican Revolution was a tendency to settle arguments with a bullet. Several of the commanding generals, as well as peasant leaders Emiliano Zapata and Pancho Villa met violent deaths, along with thousands of others. The political violence continued into the late 1920s, when former president Álvaro Obregón was shot dead in a Mexico City restaurant by a fervent Catholic supporter of the Cristero revolt opposed to his anti-clerical policies. Gradually through the 30s, institutional rule became more solid, particularly during the presidency of Lázaro Cárdenas. He put down the 1938 uprising by the former general Saturnino Cedillo in San Luis de Potosi, the last spasm of revolutionary upheaval.

Mexico's political scene has continued to have a violent undercurrent, especially during election campaigns. In 1994 the PRI's Luis Donaldo Colosio was assassinated on the campaign trail when he was the frontrunner for the upcoming presidential elections. A few months later, the president of the party Ruiz Massieu was also gunned down in a Mexico City restaurant. President Salinas's elder brother Raúl was soon arrested for having planned the murder of the person who had once been his brother-in-law. This was seen as a symptom of the tensions within the PRI as to whether it should allow an opposition party to win power or not. Neither of these murders has been properly clarified.

The Salinas brothers

In January 1999, Raúl Salinas de Gortari was sentenced to 50 years in prison for masterminding the murder. This was later cut in half by the Mexican appeals court, and then in June 2005 his conviction was quashed, and he was released from prison. He was also accused of illegal enrichment after his wife was arrested in Geneva attempting to withdraw $84 million from an account held by him under a false name. The Swiss authorities discovered he had bank accounts totalling some $110 million in their country. In 2008, $74 million was returned to the Mexican government.

Ex-president Carlos Salinas meanwhile left Mexico soon after the end of his term in office. He took refuge first in Ireland, drawn by his love of horse-racing, and later in London.

This violent way of settling political disputes is also endemic in the Mexican countryside, where local *caciques* have often recruited private armies to settle land disputes and political rivalries. However, it was with the spectacular growth of the production and trafficking of illegal drugs that violence and deaths in rural Mexico reached new levels. From the 1990s on, after the death of the Colombian drug cartel boss Pablo Escobar and the fragmentation of the drug cartels there, Mexico took over as the centre of the production and export of cocaine, heroin, methamphetamines, and marijuana, supplying markets in the United States and Europe. The trade in illegal drugs is said to generate profits of anything between $15 billion and $50 billion annually.

The fight between the different regional cartels in Mexico became increasingly bloody as they battled for control of the industry. Not only were rivals shot, but they were often decapitated as a warning, or their bodies completely dissolved in acid. The number of people killed rose dramatically through the 1990s and into the 21st century. In the cities and states where the drug gangs operate, all the institutions, from the police, the justice system, local politicians, and civil servants, as well as the press and journalists, come under threat.

Drugs and corruption

The Mexican state's response to this has been continually undermined by widespread corruption among the many different levels of police forces and political authorities. Added to this are the impunity with which crimes are committed (only 3 per cent of murders ever lead to anyone being put on trial) and also perhaps a feeling among the population that things are all right as long as the deaths are mostly among the traffickers and their gangs rather than ordinary citizens – although in fact this has never been the case.

This drugs-related violence became such a threat to public law and order that in 2006 the incoming PAN president Felipe Calderón declared what he called 'open war' on the drug cartels. Unable to trust the police, he controversially brought in the armed forces, above all the navy marines, to patrol rural areas and cities and arrest or kill gang leaders and members. The strategy of trying to capture or eliminate cartel leaders backfired: losing their bosses, the cartels tended to fragment, leading to even more violence as the smaller groups fought to win control of the trade in their regions.

Ayotzinapa

The event which brought home to many Mexicans just how out of control this drug trafficking violence had become was the 2014 massacre of 43 students from the Ayotzinapa agricultural college near the town of Iguala in Guerrero state. The students had taken over three buses, which they wanted to have driven to Mexico City to take part in commemorations of the 2 October 1968 massacre in Tlatelolco Square. On the night of 26 September 2014 they were forced off the buses, abducted, and never seen or heard of again.

What exactly happened that night has never been properly investigated, but journalists who interviewed local people say that municipal, state, and federal police forces violently intercepted the students and then handed them over to members of an illegal drugs gang, the Guerreros Unidos, who killed all 43 and buried their bodies in a mass grave. The local mayor and his wife were implicated, accused of ordering the initial arrest of the students. The local police chief was also arrested, and the state governor was forced to resign. Federal government investigations have so far failed to come up with any convincing explanation of what happened, who was responsible, or what exactly happened to the bodies. One investigative journalist has convincingly argued that, without the students' knowledge, two of the hijacked buses contained large hidden amounts of heroin, and that a local drug cartel boss ordered the colonel of the 27th Army Infantry Battalion to intercept the buses.

This event became a national and international scandal. It brought home to many Mexicans how dysfunctional the state was on all levels: from the municipal police to the state authorities, and to the federal legal and justice systems, who once again failed to bring any of those behind the murders to justice.

Migrant murders

The armed gangs not only deal in the production and marketing of illicit drugs, but also run rackets in extortion, kidnapping, blackmail, and other crimes. Particularly shocking in recent years has been the involvement of these gangs in the murder of Central American migrants whom they smuggle through Mexico as they try to reach the United States and the dream of a better life in that country. Once again, specific incidents revealed to many Mexicans that this kind of crime was rife in their country. In April 2011, as many as 193 bodies were unearthed from 47 mass graves at San Fernando in Tamaulipas state, most of them with their skulls crushed. It is thought they had been forced off buses, held for ransom, and whether that was paid or not, brutally murdered. Some press reports said the male victims had been forced to fight each other gladiator style, with the winner being incorporated into Los Zetas criminal gang.

In fact, this was the second massacre in San Fernando. A year earlier, in August 2010, the bodies of 72 migrants were found, also apparently forced off buses, held in clandestine locations, and then murdered. These two incidents gruesomely demonstrated how Central American migrants passing through Mexico endured not only a lack of safety and security and repeated violations of their human rights, but also a lack of commitment by the authorities to address these crimes. It took three years for the National Human Rights Commission to issue a report showing that the investigations and handling of the bodies were characterized by negligence and errors, but then the commission failed to issue any opinion regarding the violations of the right to life and physical safety of individuals who find themselves in Mexican territory.

Huachicoleo

Another area that organized gangs have moved into was dramatically illustrated on 19 January 2019. A PEMEX pipeline near the town of Tlahuelilpan in Hidalgo state, north of Mexico City, exploded, killing more than 130 people. The oil from the pipeline was being siphoned off and sold by criminals to locals. Fumes from the leak saturated the surrounding air and created a huge fireball that ignited, setting the surrounding fields on fire.

This tragedy brought national and international attention to a crime that in 2018 was said to have cost the Mexican state $3 billion. For years, criminal gangs had joined forces with corrupt politicians (and often with PEMEX officials) to siphon off fuel from the main pipelines and sell it cheaply to local inhabitants. The AMLO administration had already begun to crack down on fuel oil thefts, known locally as '*huachicoleo*', after the slang term for illegal liquor. By the end of 2018, when he came into office, these thefts were said to be running at more than three million gallons a day. The most spectacular of these was the loss of some 1.5 million gallons from one illegal pipeline tap in a single day.

AMLO made it a top priority of his new security minister to send federal security forces to patrol the most affected areas and arrest anyone suspected of involvement. He also ordered several of the most frequently targeted pipelines to be shut down altogether, leading to fuel shortages in several states. The response of the criminal gangs was immediate and violent. Roads into the city of Guanajuato were blocked; a bomb was planted in a truck outside a major refinery; a federal attorney general's office was raked with gunfire; and AMLO himself received death threats.

By April 2019 AMLO was able to claim victory, announcing 'we managed to defeat the fuel thieves.' According to PEMEX, thefts had decreased in four months to some 170,000 gallons per day. The challenge for the government now is on the one hand to continue with the crackdown rather than to consider the problem solved, and also to alleviate poverty in those areas where residents have welcomed the gangs both because of the cheap petrol they offered, and the largesse they often showered on the local population.

The gang-related violence is most evident in border cities such as Tijuana, in the north-west of Mexico opposite San Diego in the United States. In 2018 a record number of 2,518 murders were recorded in this city of fewer than 2 million inhabitants, 90 per cent of them said to be murders related to battles between different criminal gangs fighting for control of the synthetic drugs market.

Ciudad Juárez

At the other end of the border, Ciudad Juárez, opposite the Texan city of El Paso, became notorious in recent years for a huge spate of femicides. The huge increase in the killing of women in the city appears to have started in 1993. By 2005, some 370 corpses of murdered women had been found; by 2010, at the peak of this phenomenon, the reported figure for that year alone was 247 in Ciudad Juárez. The majority of the victims were poor young workers from the *maquiladoras* (assembly plants) that provide cheap goods for the United States and are the main source of employment in the border region. Often, the murdered women had migrated from other Mexican states to the border area, where the fact that they lacked any family ties or close friendships made them more vulnerable. Once again, the presence of organized drug gangs in the area has been seen as one of the main causes behind this upsurge of deaths. The denunciation of these femicides led to international pressure on the Mexican authorities to conduct proper investigations and bring those responsible to court. But, as with other violent crimes, the official response has been negligible: only three people have been put on trial for these murders.

The seemingly unending crisis of killings linked to the illegal drugs trade was one of the most pressing issues facing President López Obrador when he took office in December 2018. That year saw close to 70,000 people murdered in Mexico, a grisly record. AMLO's response so far has been weak and inadequate. During his campaign he spoke of a 'hugs not bullets' approach to the violence, but the continuing bloody warfare (a homicide rate of 27 per 100,000 inhabitants) soon forced him to change tack.

A vivid example of the Mexican state's inability to properly confront the gangs came with the failed arrest of Ovidio Guzmán López, the son of the infamous cartel leader Joaquín Guzmán Loera, known as 'El Chapo'. After twice escaping from prison in Mexico, El Chapo was extradited to the United States in 2019, and is currently serving a lengthy sentence for drug trafficking and other crimes. His son Guzmán López was taken into custody in October 2019 in the city of Culiacán, in the state of Sinaloa, one of the main centres for the illegal drugs trade in the western coastal region. The response of his gang members was so ferocious that the city was closed off, and the detachment of soldiers sent to arrest him found themselves surrounded and outgunned. So desperate was their situation that the AMLO government agreed to López Guzmán's release in return for a guarantee that the National Guardsmen not be harmed. López Guzmán has not been recaptured.

The National Guard

The creation of the National Guard has been AMLO's main initiative in the fight against the cartels. His predecessors had increasingly turned to the armed forces, especially the navy marines, to be the front line of the fight against the drug gangs. Corruption among the many different police forces charged with keeping law and order had been widespread for so many years it was argued that only a properly trained elite force created out of armed forces' personnel could be relied on to do the job. This ignored the evidence that large numbers of highly trained soldiers changed sides and became part of ruthless drug gangs such as Los Zetas.

During his election campaign, AMLO promised he would end the involvement of the military in this struggle. This promise reflected the deep mistrust most Mexicans have felt ever since the revolution early in the 20th century over allowing the armed forces any role in law enforcement within the country, as this is seen as a threat to democratic civilian rule.

The army's role

Unlike many other Latin American countries the Mexican army (about 185,000 strong) has largely stayed out of politics since the 1930s. The then president Lázaro Cárdenas made the military one of the four corporate entities in the newly created National Revolutionary Party (which was to evolve into the PRI), along with labour, popular organizations, and rural groups. This move coincided with the replacement of those high-ranking officers who had lived through the revolution (known as the *mustangs*) with younger ones more interested in a soldiering career. The solidity of the institutions created by the PRI, and the continuing respect for the six-year presidential and legislative terms, has meant that the Mexican armed forces have in the main had little to do with political life, and were kept out of the kind of brutal repression of the civilian population so prevalent in much of the rest of the continent.

There were several exceptions to this. In 1968, widespread student protests against the government took place over months in Mexico City and elsewhere. On 2 October 1968, only a few weeks prior to the opening of the Olympic Games, special forces from the Mexican army are said to have killed as many as 300 people holding a mass demonstration in Tlatelolco Square in the north of the capital. Many hundreds more were arrested and held as political prisoners in the infamous Lecumberri prison in the centre of the city. The PRI government managed to weather the political and social storm this massacre created. The Olympic Games were staged as normal, and the armed forces returned to their barracks, while a myth grew up around these events that paralleled the one in France after the May 1968 *événements*.

Apart from this urban unrest, the most serious guerrilla threat to institutional rule came in the early 1970s in the mountainous region in the state of Guerrero, where Lucio Cabañas emerged as the leader of the Ejercito de los Pobres (Army of the Poor). President Echeverria sent both the paramilitary *Halcones* and army troops to combat the threat, and after Cabañas was killed in 1974 the guerrilla movement faded away. But during this campaign, as elsewhere on the continent, the Mexican army was accused of using the illegal tactics of a 'dirty war': executions, clandestine prisons, torture, and disappearances.

The third most striking instance of the Mexican armed forces being used to quell internal unrest has been their deployment in Chiapas to confront the EZLN. Formed in the 1980s when survivors from the small middle-class urban guerrillas struck an alliance with indigenous communities in the far southern Lacandón jungle area of Chiapas, by the 1990s the EZLN had grown into a considerable force. When the Zapatistas launched their uprising on 1 January 1994, led by the legendary Subcomandante Marcos, they took over several towns, including the tourist centre San Cristóbal de las Casas. In response, President Salinas sent some 12,000 troops to combat the threat. The armed conflict against the Zapatistas went on for 12 days, leading to as many as 300 deaths, and many thousands of reports of human rights violations.

After two years of negotiations, an uneasy peace was restored thanks to the San Andrés accords, but these were undermined in December 1997 at the village of Acteal when an armed group killed 45 men, women, and children regarded as Zapatista supporters, while nearby police and army units ignored what was going on. Since then army personnel have continued to be deployed in Chiapas, but there have been no incursions into the territory claimed by the EZLN and the indigenous groups supporting them.

In addition to these examples of the Mexican armed forces being used against their own people, there have been many cases of corrupt practices, and protection of the drug gangs at the highest levels. The most notorious of these was the case of General Jesús Gutiérrez Rebollo, who was the Zedillo government's anti-drugs 'czar' in the second half of the 1990s. To the Mexican authorities' great embarrassment, it was the US Drugs Enforcement Agency (DEA) that provided them with convincing evidence that Rebollo was taking bribes from the Juárez drug cartel and its leader Amado Carrillo Fuentes in return for tip-offs and protection. This created such a scandal within Mexico and internationally that the general was arrested, put on trial, and sentenced to 40 years in jail. He died there in 2013.

All of this explains why AMLO was so reluctant to continue to use the armed forces to fight the cartels on the streets of Mexico. However, it only took him two months in office to perform a volte-face and declare his intention of setting up an elite National Guard to do precisely that. By May 2019 as many as 60,000 personnel drawn from the federal police, the army police, and special navy forces had been recruited for this new force.

Almost from its inception, the role of the National Guard appears to have been distorted. As part of the accord with US President Donald Trump and his 'Remain in Mexico' plan, which insisted that the Mexican government step up its efforts to prevent central American migrants crossing the country and attempting to enter the United States without papers, AMLO agreed to deploy a large proportion of the newly formed guard to patrol the southern border with Guatemala and turn back any immigrants attempting to enter Mexico.

This has inevitably led to a weakening of the National Guard's efforts to combat organized crime, producing fiascos such as the botched attempt to arrest El Chapo's son. Like his predecessors, AMLO has yet to find a convincing short-term strategy to reduce the levels of violence and to provide justice for the victims, as well as longer term solutions to the levels of poverty and lack of different opportunities for many people in rural areas. Nor does there seem to be any solution to the problem of drug consumption in the United States and elsewhere. As long as there is such an inexhaustible market so close by, Mexicans seem doomed to continue to suffer from the violence and corruption related to the illegal trade.

10 Conclusion: The fourth transformation

The 21st century has seen enormous changes in the political life of Mexico. Three very different parties have occupied the Eagle Throne that is the symbol of presidential authority. But many Mexicans wonder if these changes at the top represent a true deepening of democratic rule in their country. Until the arrival of MORENA and AMLO to the presidency, they were treated to the strange spectacle of 12 years of the main opposition party finally coming to power, but failing to grasp the opportunity to make the much-needed reforms to the way Mexico is run.

After 12 years in the wilderness, the PRI returned, with President Peña Nieto promising a 'pact for all Mexicans' and attempting to usher in long overdue reform in areas such as state-run industries, education, and the judiciary. Tensions within his own party led to a stalemate, and so dismayed voters that they were willing to give an outsider like AMLO a chance.

The PRI, the party that 'institutionalized' the revolution and managed to achieve a degree of social cohesion for many years, has found it hard to accept that it is simply a political party like all the others, and needs to present credible policies and alternatives if it is to be returned to power. The level of discredit into which it has fallen is starkly illustrated by the damning list of failures offered by the Mexican sociologist Roger Bartra (in *La Sombra del Futuro*): 'it is the party that most obviously symbolizes impunity, electoral fraud, disrespect for the law, the manipulation and diversion of public funds'.

The right-wing PAN meanwhile proved during its 12 years in power that it was happy to embrace the neo-liberal economic policies pursued by the PRI, as these favoured its core base of middle and upper class urban Mexicans. However, it did little to seize the opportunity to undertake fundamental reforms that would have significantly changed the deeply ingrained political system. It appeared far too content simply to continue with the *status quo*, and so lost the support of many voters.

The arrival of AMLO and the sweeping victory of his MORENA party at all levels of federal and regional government generated hopes that this time there could be a radical transformation of Mexican society. At first, foreign and local investors were worried that AMLO, whom they considered a firebrand left-wing popular leader, might seek to buy support by massively increasing public spending. The Mexican stock market fell sharply, and the Mexican peso came under pressure.

To many people's surprise, AMLO did the opposite. Arguing for 'republican austerity' he cut public sector wages and made a start on rooting out corruption and increasing efficiency in state enterprises. He kept control of fiscal spending, aiming to balance the budget. AMLO began his presidency in a rush, typified by his daily early morning briefings that many journalists struggled to attend. He refused to move into the lavish presidential mansion of Los Pinos in Chapultepec Park, and had it turned into a cultural centre. His first cabinet of ministers contained the same number of women as men. He increased pensions for several million Mexicans, set minimum prices for several of the country's staple crops, and brought in scholarships and apprenticeships for more than a million young people.

AMLO also attempted to broaden participation in political decisions by making repeated use of *consultas populares* or votes open to everyone on major initiatives he was proposing. Opposition parties denounced this as cheap populism, and criticized his launching of several mega-projects such as the Tren Maya, the change of plans for a new Mexico City international airport, and the Dos Bocas oil refinery in his home state of Tabasco.

He also lost support due to what was seen by many Mexicans as a failure to stand up to US President Donald Trump. Not only did he agree to curb the flow of Mexicans trying to cross the border into the United States, but he diverted the newly created National Guard (in itself a controversial move) into patrolling Mexico's southern frontier in order to keep out Central American migrants also trying to reach the United States.

At the same time, the number of Mexicans killed in the drug wars increased yet again in 2019–2020. AMLO rejected the idea of an 'all-out war' on the drugs cartels and his predecessors' strategy of trying to capture the 'kingpins' of the different organizations.

Instead, he emphasized the need to do away with corruption and the rural poverty that led people to work for the cartels. Neither of these long-term goals offered ordinary Mexicans the promise of any respite from the day-to-day violence that could occur in almost any of the 32 states. Above all, the MORENA president faced criticism and the accusation of indulging in 'retropopulism' by seeking to make the huge state-run PEMEX oil and gas company the centre of efforts to boost government revenues, when most experts think it is far too unwieldy and mired in corruption to be turned around in this way. AMLO also sought to increase state control on the electricity industry, including in the area of the promotion of alternatives to fossil fuels. To many local observers, this looked like an attempt to turn the clock back, and to recreate the kind of society that had proved successful for the PRI for many years, but had eventually collapsed.

Early in 2020, AMLO and his government were confronted by a crisis no one had bargained for. By mid-August 2020, the Covid-19 pandemic had led to more than 55,000 deaths in Mexico; the president was widely attacked for his apparently relaxed approach to the disease. While he appeared unconcerned, tourism collapsed, manufacturing, especially in the maquila sector, was massively hit by the recession in the United States, and remittances also suffered badly. Experts forecast that Mexico's GDP could contract by 9 per cent or more in 2020, with at least a million workers facing unemployment. Once again, however, AMLO chose not to greatly increase government spending to counteract the worst effects of the pandemic, seemingly unwilling to increase the country's indebtedness.

This may only worsen the recession, and as AMLO reaches the second half of his term in office (due to end in 2024) he faces the choice of loosening the purse strings (as successive PRI administrations used to do) if he wishes to persuade Mexicans to continue to vote for his MORENA party, or risk widespread discontent and the return of one of the other two main political parties if he continues with his austerity policies.

For the moment, both the PRI and the PAN are weakened by the failures of their recent terms in office and internal struggles. They appear unable to mount a serious challenge to his government, which controls nearly all the states and has a majority in both houses of the national Congress. Of greater concern for him is the possible fragmentation of the coalition of left and centre groups that have backed him until now. He has little time to cement his promised 'fourth transformation' of Mexico, and make good on his promise that his would be an administration that would lift millions of Mexicans out of poverty.

Food and drink

Mexican food is famous for its variety and richness. Meat dishes, seafood, and a huge array of vegetables and fruit make it one of the world's most enticing cuisines. Maize is one of the basic ingredients in many recipes – and of course there are many kinds of *chiles* or chillies that range from hot to incandescent.

Drinks

cerveza (chela): usually a light lager type of beer
michelada: beer and lime, served with salt round the rim of the bottle or glass
parroquia coffee: espresso coffee with scalding hot milk
piña colada: pineapple juice, rum, and coconut
Pulque, mezcal, and *tequila* are all made from the agave plant. Pulque is the roughest, mezcal often has a *gusano* or worm in it, while tequila is the most refined, and traditionally comes from the town of that name near Guadalajara.
vino: wine. Mexican wine is enjoying something of a renaissance

Food

frijoles charros: pork with black beans
lentejas estilo antequera: spicy lentil stew with plantain and pineapple
mole de olla: beef stew with chillies and vegetables
pavo con mole: turkey in a honey-rich black sauce
pechuga de pollo en adobo: chicken breasts in adobo sauce

Snacks

Usually known as *antojitos*:

caldo de camarón: shrimp broth (beware of the chillies)
chilaquiles: tortilla wedges fried and then covered in a sauce

enchiladas: tortillas dipped in sauce topped with chicken or meat, covered in cheese or cream

frijoles: beans served in hundreds of different ways

huevos rancheros: fried eggs on fried tortilla, covered in tomato sauce

quesadillas: fried or grilled tortillas filled with cheese

tacos: tortillas wrapped round a variety of fillings

tamales: chicken, pork and beans in steamed maize or banana leaves

Travel basics

Trains: Trains in Mexico are very slow and most of the lines have been cut, except for a few tourist trains such as the one visiting Copper Canyon in the north. There is a vast network of usually efficient long-distance buses. Due to the lack of security in many regions, it is increasingly common for people to take one of the budget airlines to fly from city to city.

Car hire: Hiring a car is very easy and common, particularly in the main resorts. Take precautions against robbery, and it is not a good idea to drive at night or to leave a car parked out overnight. Make sure all your paperwork and insurance is in order (see comment about 'police' below).

Safety: Tourists are unlikely to be caught up in the violence surrounding the drugs trade, but petty crime is common, and the big cities have 'no-go' areas you should be aware of. Steer clear of the police, as they have a reputation for extracting bribes. It is also best not to get into a taxi with only two doors, as foreigners can find themselves 'taxi-napped' for money.

Women travellers: Mexican machismo can be a concern for women travelling on their own; single women are often regarded as available to be picked up.

Health: Usually best to avoid water from taps; mineral water is readily available. Mexico City is situated at over 8,000 feet, so beware of altitude sickness and finding it hard to breathe. Take your time. The sun can also burn at these altitudes, so a hat, sun cream, or other protection is recommended, as is travel insurance: the public health system in Mexico can be poor, and private medicine expensive.

Changing money: Banks and bureaux de change (*casas de cambio*) will change foreign currency: the *casas de cambio* generally offer better rates than banks and hotels.

Drugs: Frequently offered on the streets, but stay away from them.

Souvenirs: Mexico is one of the best countries in the world to buy handicrafts (*artesanias*) and other souvenirs. All the cities and big towns have markets which sell many different kinds of usually highly coloured items, with each region having its own specialties. The government-run Conaculta stores have a wide array of regional artefacts.

Mexicanismos

The Spanish spoken in Mexico is rich in slang and colloquial expressions, as well as terms imported from American English and Mexican indigenous languages. Young people in particular are constantly inventing new terms, but the following are among the commonest heard in conversation.

¡a huevo! you bet!
bato: man, guy
bocho (vocho): Volkswagen Beetle, until recently the commonest green taxi
buena onda: good vibes
cabrón: bastard
  A ese cabrón no le creo nada: I don't believe a word that bastard says
carnal: best friend, buddy
chamba: job
chavo/chava: boy/girl
chela: beer
chido: great/cool
chilango: someone from Mexico City
chingar/chingadera/chingada: to fuck/screw
  ¡chinga tu madre! fuck you!
compa: friend
crudo: hangover
cuate: friend
desmadre: mess
gacho: cheap/mean
güey: mate, buddy
  ¿como vas, güey? how're you doing, mate?
hijo de la chingada: son of a bitch
¡híjole! yeah, fantastic!
huevón: idiot
jeta: face
me vale madre: I couldn't give a damn

naco: tacky, kitsch
nave: car
neta: really
  es la neta: it's great
¡*no mames!* you're kidding!
órale: sure, you bet
¡*padre / que padre!* cool
pendejo: asshole
Que onda? What's up, what gives?
tianguis: market
verga: prick
  me vale verga: I couldn't give a damn

Printed in the USA
CPSIA information can be obtained
at www.ICGtesting.com
JSHW012055140824
68134JS00035B/3460